THE
Hedgewitch's
LITTLE BOOK OF
Seasonal
Magic

© Sarah Coyne

ABOUT THE AUTHOR

Tudorbeth is the principal of the British College of Witchcraft and Wizardry and teaches courses on witchcraft. She is the author of numerous books, including *A Spellbook for the Seasons* (Eddison Books, 2019). Tudorbeth is a hereditary practitioner; her great grandmother was a well-known tea reader in Ireland while her Welsh great grandmother was a healer and wise woman.

THE
Hedgewitch's
LITTLE BOOK OF
Seasonal
Magic

❧⊱•⊰❧

TUDORBETH

Llewellyn Publications
Woodbury, MN

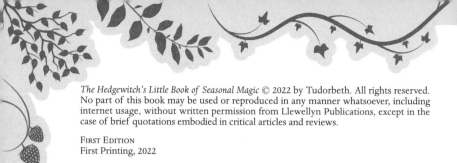

FIRST EDITION
First Printing, 2022

Book design by Donna Burch-Brown
Cover design by Shira Atakpu
Interior art by the Llewellyn Art Department

Llewellyn Publications is a registered trademark of Llewellyn Worldwide Ltd.

Library of Congress Cataloging-in-Publication Data
Names: Tudorbeth, author.
Title: The hedgewitch's little book of seasonal magic / Tudorbeth.
Description: First edition. | Woodbury, MN : Llewellyn Publications, 2022.
 | Includes bibliographical references.
Identifiers: LCCN 2021050972 (print) | LCCN 2021050973 (ebook) | ISBN
 9780738769929 (hardcover) | ISBN 9780738770055 (ebook)
Subjects: LCSH: Magic. | Witchcraft. | Seasons—Miscellanea.
Classification: LCC BF1611 .T83 2022 (print) | LCC BF1611 (ebook) | DDC
 133.4/3—dc23/eng/20211104
LC record available at https://lccn.loc.gov/2021050972
LC ebook record available at https://lccn.loc.gov/2021050973

Llewellyn Worldwide Ltd. does not participate in, endorse, or have any authority or responsibility concerning private business transactions between our authors and the public.
 All mail addressed to the author is forwarded but the publisher cannot, unless specifically instructed by the author, give out an address or phone number.
 Any internet references contained in this work are current at publication time, but the publisher cannot guarantee that a specific location will continue to be maintained. Please refer to the publisher's website for links to authors' websites and other sources.

Llewellyn Publications
A Division of Llewellyn Worldwide Ltd.
2143 Wooddale Drive
Woodbury, MN 55125-2989
www.llewellyn.com

Printed in the United States of America

DEDICATION

Dedicated to all those who believe in magic and practice it freely. May your strength inspire us all.

Blessed be.

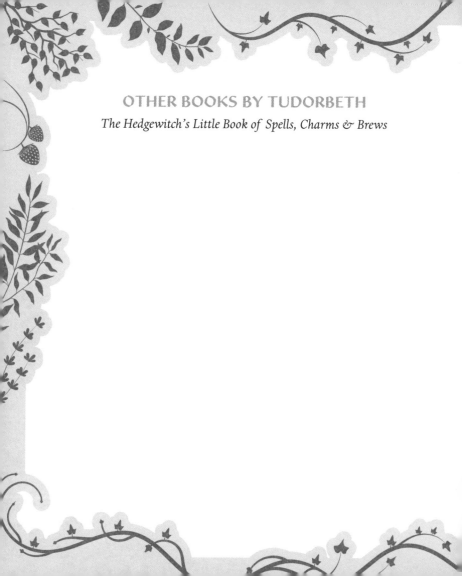

OTHER BOOKS BY TUDORBETH

The Hedgewitch's Little Book of Spells, Charms & Brews

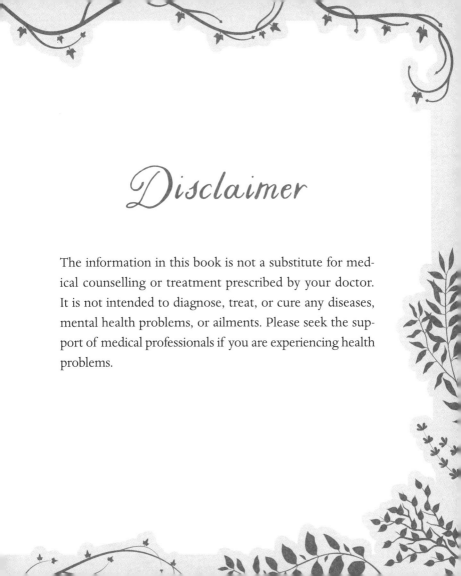

Disclaimer

The information in this book is not a substitute for medical counselling or treatment prescribed by your doctor. It is not intended to diagnose, treat, or cure any diseases, mental health problems, or ailments. Please seek the support of medical professionals if you are experiencing health problems.

Contents

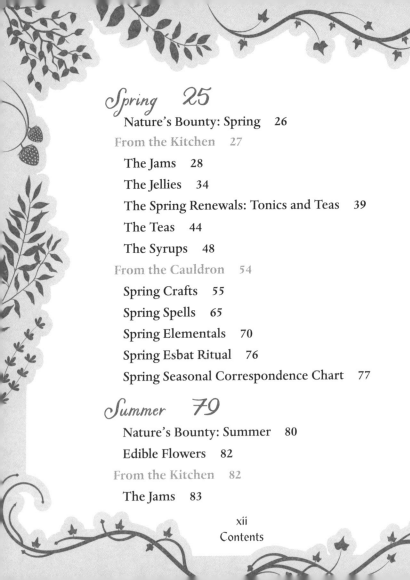

Autumn   133

Winter   181

Introduction

Hedgewitchery is just one small branch on the giant tree of Paganism. It can be found within the realms of witchcraft and is often viewed as a solitary practitioner's path. Hedgewitchery is deeply esoteric and embedded within nature. Although witchcraft in general is a nature-based religion, hedgewitchery seems to stand alone in its views as no two hedgewitches practice exactly in the same way. This is due to the very isolated and individual way hedgewitchery approaches the year and the seasons.

The best way to describe a hedgewitch is a folklorist or a follower of nature craft. Plants, trees, wildlife, and the environment hold a sacred place in a hedgewitch's heart, as do weather phenomena, but there are many core beliefs that set a hedgewitch apart from their other Wiccan siblings.

First, they do not adhere to Wicca; second, they do not have a bespoke ritual to follow; third, they do not engage in a coven; and last, hedgewitches generally do not engage in affairs of the world. First and foremost, hedgewitches protect, help, and heal flora and fauna, including the elemental energies that live in our worlds.

In this book, you will find several spells and practices that are from a Celtic hedgewitch, and yet, if you were to seek an Australian hedgewitch, they would do things slightly differently. This is because hedgewitchery is determined by the environment the hedgewitch finds themself in and which culture they stem from. We all have a go-to herb or plant or dish that is used in healing, spell-weaving, and/or curing. For example, in Italy, the herb is basil; in my culture, it is the nettle; in an Australian hedgewitch's pantry, it could be eucalyptus.

Magic and witchcraft are around us all in so many ways, from lighting a candle and making a wish on a birthday cake, to Valentine's Day's pink-and-red cards. Wishing on a candle is one of the oldest forms of magic known: it is candle magic. The cards covered in pinks and reds are synonymous with the thoughts and feelings of love. This colour association forms part of our basic language, otherwise known as correspondences.

The correspondences are like our alphabet, and although other witches do adhere to them, for the hedgewitch, they are paramount to everything we do and how we live. The correspondences are infinite, and with each new generation they grow further, but their origins are deep within the earth and universe, and this is what hedgewitches adhere to: the beginning, as it were.

Therefore, in this book, you will find recipes, spells, and potions with nature very much at their heart. All manner of natural resources will be used, and that includes the weather on some occasions. This book will follow the sun around its seasonal year and will generally have the same subjects for each season. However, there are seasonal differences in the ingredients and specific craft projects you can make. Also, the seasons themselves dictate to us what we can create. For example, there are tonics and teas in spring, whereas in autumn, we concentrate on making chutneys. This is because the spring herbs and plants are bursting with new life, which can have a healthy effect, whereas with the onset of autumn, our attention turns more to preservation of the fruits and essentially stocking up for winter. Further, there are some generic instructions featured throughout all the seasons, and they can be found in the next section. In each season, there are also an Esbat ritual and a seasonal correspondence chart. An Esbat is a bit like our sabbath, but instead of every week, we perform it once a month, coinciding with the full moon. Furthermore, this book contains recipes, craft ideas, spells, and elemental beings who are the cornerstone of a hedgewitch's path.

Hedgewitchery may go against your realistic belief system of Darwinian science, and if that is the case, then this book is not for you. Always trust your instincts, as this branch of the Craft (witchcraft) is not for everyone. Further, this branch has its origins in hereditary witchcraft: recipes, sayings, and spells, both healing and defensive. But first and foremost, the hedgewitch is the solitary, nature-protecting, and esoteric witch.

Traditionally, the hedgewitch was a female, but times are changing, and the magic of the Craft is that it can adapt to needs and wants of the world. The hedgewitch can now be any gender. The Craft accepts all, as we are all magical.

The very essence of the hedgewitch is the rider of realms—the witch who travels to two lands: the world we see around us, and the one we do not. That other realm communes with Earth energies known as elemental beings. And we are not just talking about the fae, but also other energies whose presence in the everyday world is experienced through cobwebs on the face, taps on the shoulders, orbs, flashes of light, cats watching and following the movement of empty space, or dogs barking at nothing.

Hedgewitchery is the creaking of stairs and the whispering of leaves in a city park. It is the world of missing keys, falling feathers, and objects moving and appearing in strange places—the smell of flowers where there are none to be seen, or the scent of cinnamon when no one is baking. It is owls in the night and strange music carried on the breeze.

This is nature.

This is our Earth.

Welcome to the world of the hedgewitch.

The Hedgewitch's Supplies

When it comes to equipment, hedgewitches dislike throwing anything out and will always try to reuse something. There are a number of utensils and resources that will be used in every season, and they are as follows.

JAM JARS

This valuable resource is cheap and environmentally friendly, so start saving all your glass jars and make sure they have a top to go with them. Always wash them out completely and remove labels, and if using them to make jams or chutneys, sterilise them before use.

Traditional Sterilising

Wash jars and their lids in warm soapy water and then rinse. Leave them upside down on a draining board; do not dry them. Put them on a tray with the lids and place them in a preheated oven at 160°C/320°F–180°C/350°F for about fifteen to twenty minutes.

Ladle the preserve into the jars using a special heat-proof funnel or jug. Leave about a ¼-inch or ½-centimeter gap between the preserve and the lid.

As soon as the hot contents are in, cover with a piece of wax paper or cellophane and then securely fasten the lid. As the mixture cools, the lids will start popping as they seal themselves.

Use smaller jars for jellies, as you would not use as much jelly as jam or marmalade. Plus, they look *très chic* when given as a gift of two or three.

GLASS BOTTLES

Start saving your glass bottles as well, especially all different sizes and colours, as these are particularly good for bath and massage oils. If you intend to make different types of alcoholic beverages, these are great to give as presents.

Once again, wash in warm soapy water, removing the labels, and make sure to wash the lids. Rinse and leave on a draining board. Place all bottles and lids on a tray and place in a preheated oven at around 170°C/330°F for fifteen minutes before taking them out and leaving them to cool slightly while you sieve the alcoholic beverage. Pop the lid on and leave before labelling.

The Hedgewitch's Cupboard

These key ingredients are important and versatile in a hedgewitch's pantry. They are food items that can be used for culinary purposes, but they are equally beneficial medicinally and magically.

In addition to these seven food items, there are a number of key herbs that are useful to have in your cupboard. These, too, have properties and uses that benefit culinary, medicinal, and magical pursuits.

THE SEVEN KEY INGREDIENTS

Salt

Salt is probably the most important ingredient a hedge-witch can have in the cupboard. It can be used for so many things, including healing and spell-weaving, purification, consecration, and, of course, cooking. There are many different types of salt, too, and it can come in many different colours, from pink Himalayan salt, to white sea salt, to the black lava salt of Hawaii.

Salt represents the five elements: it comes from the sea and therefore is water; it is found in the earth and mined; it is dried in the air; and if you put a piece on your tongue, it burns, thus it is also fire. It is also pure and therefore represents divinity. It is a natural resource that is fundamental to life—it is crucial for life, and yet too much of it is dangerous.

The best salt to have in your hedgewitch cupboard is a good sea salt in any of its forms, such as flakes or rocks or finely ground grains. Any of those is fine, and as it is white, it will go with any dish or recipe or spell intent.

Sugar

Sugar is another fundamental ingredient to life and is a vital resource to have in any hedgewitch's cupboard. Once again, there are different forms of sugar, from refined white sugar, to brown sugar, to demerara sugar, to icing sugar, to loose sugar, to sugar cubes. The best sugar to have is white granulated sugar; this is used in every household dish, from tea to cakes.

Honey

Honey is a sacred product made by bees, who are revered in hedgewitchery. In many ancient cultures, bees have often been described as deities and given high status in the lands they inhabit. From ancient Egypt to Mesoamerica, bees are sacred beings who command respect, and the product they make is often believed to be a gift from the gods themselves. Honey for a Celtic hedgewitch is regarded as a blessing, and having it in the house both protects and blesses it.

Honey has many purposes aside from cooking or sweetening tea. It also has healing properties. For example, honey stirred in a cup of hot water with lemon and ginger can help with colds and flu. Honey has antibacterial and antifungal properties and is a good source of antioxidants. Up until the last century, people were known to use it on wounds to help heal and cure.

Any form of honey is ideal to have in your hedgewitch cupboard, especially if it is locally produced, and make sure to never run out of it.

Olive Oil

Another gift from the gods, the glorious olive and the oil made from it are beneficial to the health of humans. Olive oil can be used for almost anything, from cooking, to healing, to even beauty regimes. My own grandmother used it as a moisturiser for her infant son, and until the day he passed, my father's skin was glowing, with no wrinkles or blemishes ever. Olive oil has large amounts of antioxidants, anti-inflammatory properties, and vitamin E, which are all ideal for healthy hair and skin.

The best type of olive oil to have in the hedgewitchery cupboard is extra virgin olive oil, as this is the least processed or refined type of olive oil.

Butter

For many years, butter was regarded as the enemy. However, new data is finding what we in witchcraft have always known: butter, like all things taken in moderation, is actually rather healthy for you. It has many minerals in it, such as selenium and vitamins D, E, and K. It has also been discovered that the saturated fats in butter may have properties that fight tumours and cancer.[1]

The best type of butter to have is pure organic butter. Always try to have the organic or purest type of any ingredient in your cupboard.

Wine

Wine is used for many things, including rituals, cooking, and healing a nauseous stomach. It changes during the

1. Sally Fallon and Mary G. Enig, "Why Butter Is Better," *The Weston A. Price Foundation*, January 1, 2000, https://www.westonaprice.org /health-topics/know-your-fats/why-butter-is-better/.

seasons: red is best for autumn and winter, while white is best for spring and summer. However, if you do not have alcohol in your house, a perfect substitute is grape juice (red grape juice for autumn and winter, white grape juice for spring and summer). Nonalcoholic wine is also a good alternative, and both can be used in any recipe, spell, or ritual that requires wine.

Vinegar

Vinegar is one of those key resources we always should have in our hedgewitch's cupboard. It can be used for so many things, from cooking, to cleaning, to healing, to killing weeds, cleaning pots, preserving cut flowers, germinating seeds, and increasing soil acidity, as well as a whole range of other garden benefits. Vinegar, like salt, is an all-rounder and does so much.

The ideal vinegar to have in your cupboard is apple cider vinegar with "mother," which is the combination of yeast and bacteria that is formed during fermentation. This is the best type of vinegar as it is unpasteurised, and unfiltered apple cider vinegar will probably be organic.

HERBS

Rosemary

Rosemary is probably the most versatile herb around and can be grown anywhere. In the Mediterranean, its natural home, it is used as hedges and grows freely. Its distinctive flavour adds warmth to meat and chicken dishes especially, but equally it can be used in magic. It is used in a range of spells and rituals, from money, to health, to career and protection spells. It is particularly good for enhancing good luck, and many people also use it in remembrance rituals for deceased loved ones. In England, it was customary to place three sprigs of rosemary on the coffins and graves of the recently deceased as a sign of remembrance and love.

Lavender

Lavender is an herb that is often overlooked for its culinary properties. This is a shame, as it is delicious in biscuits and cookies. It also makes soothing summer drinks, both alcoholic and nonalcoholic. A couple of flower heads placed in sugar or salt and left in a sealed jar creates lavender salt or sugar, which can then be used for culinary, medicinal, and magical practices and dishes. Medicinally, this herb can be used for mental health, especially for stress and insomnia. Magically, it can be used in love, family, and healing spells.

Mint

Mint is such a versatile herb. It can be added to drinks (both alcoholic and nonalcoholic), make sweets and desserts, and be a flavour in the main dish. However, though we may think of mint as predominantly a culinary herb, it is equally beneficial in medicinal and magical practices. Mint has been used for thousands of years to ease stomach complaints, such as nausea, indigestion, and sickness. It is ideal for the digestive system as it is believed to increase and encourage bile flow, which helps speed and ease digestion. It can also ease headaches and cramps. Further, mint can ease a sore throat when used as a mouthwash.

Magically, mint is particularly good with money, cleansing, consecration, dream work, happiness, healing, protection, and passion spells, to name just a few. It is used for all types of prosperity spell workings, including those for career enhancement and job promotion.

Thyme

There are over fifty varieties of thyme, all with different flavours and fragrances. It grows freely anywhere and is used in many culinary dishes. It is perfect in both meat and cheese dishes and can enhance summer drinks and winter desserts. Medicinally, thyme is often used for cold and flu symptoms, such as sore throat and bronchitis, though it can also be used for stomach complaints and skin disorders. Magically, it is a good all-rounder, as it is used for spells and rituals concerning protection, enhancing good luck, and cleansing. It is also used as a consecration herb and for attracting elemental beings during Esbat rituals.

Basil

Basil is a wonderful herb for many dishes and drinks and is especially good in vegetarian and vegan dishes, where it can enhance the flavours of the other ingredients. It is especially good when used as a stomach tonic (infuse basil leaves in boiled water, leave to cool, and then drink as and when required). Alternatively, if suffering from an upset stomach, eating a couple of washed, fresh leaves can ease symptoms. Magically, basil is used for all manner of spells and rituals, including those for love, money, luck, protection, and family.

Magical Timing

PHASES OF THE MOON

Following the moon cycles is one of the main ways we plan our magic, as each phase of the moon holds a special meaning:

New Moon: Beginnings; the beginning of a new project.

Waxing: Growing and expansion.

Full Moon: Completion of a project or a relationship.

Waning: Eliminating; banishing something away from you. Waning can also mean decreasing in size.

In addition, the seasons bring their own intents: spring is for renewal; summer, healing of Earth; autumn, giving thanks for the harvest; and winter, the return of the sun.

The full moon can occur at any time during the month—beginning, middle, or end. A good way of planning your month is to use a reputable calendar that includes all the important lunar dates.[2]

FESTIVALS OF THE YEAR

Our world is magnificent—a spinning rock that glows blue throughout the blackness of space, and although she is incredibly fragile, her strength and wonder hold no bounds. And while one half of her freezes in the cold northern hemisphere, the other side is scorching under the southern sun. As such, our kin on the other side of the world follow the wheel of the year in opposite festivals, and like two sides of the same coin, we are different, but we are all one despite our differences. Here is a list of our festivals. Although many hedgewitches refer to these using different names, I have used the names that are most prominent within the Craft.[3]

....

2. *Llewellyn's Witches' Calendar* is ideal for this and includes planting and harvesting references.
3. *Hedgewitch's Little Book of Spells, Charms & Brews* (Llewellyn Publications, 2021).

Festival	Traditional Dates: Southern Hemisphere (S) Northern Hemisphere (N)
Lughnasadh/Lammas (S) Imbolc (N)	February 2
Mabon (Autumnal Equinox) (S) Ostara (N)	March 21
Samhain (S) Beltane (N)	April 30/May 1
Yule (Winter Solstice) (S) Litha (Summer Solstice) (N)	June 21
Imbolc (S) Lammas (N)	August 2
Ostara (Vernal/Spring Equinox) (S) Mabon (N)	September 21
Beltane (S) Samhain (N)	October 31
Litha (Summer Solstice) (S) Yule (Winter Solstice) (N)	December 21

ESBATS

Along with the festivals, we celebrate the Esbat, our sabbath. It is a time to give thanks and outline our plans for the coming months. It is done on the night of the full moon and lasts for three nights. Traditionally, one night is for healing, one night for thanking, and one night for casting a spell or intent for something.

The ritual of an Esbat can be something as simple as making a celebratory meal or lighting a candle. Our lives are terribly busy, and sometimes we just haven't got the time to wander off into the woods to perform a magnificent ceremony. We have work and childcare priorities, so don't worry, and never think you are being a lazy hedgewitch for not performing an Esbat. Magic, and especially hedgewitchery, is an entirely individual religion, and no one should tell you how to live it. What follows are just my ways and ideas of how I live as a hedgewitch in the modern world.

Spring

Spring is a busy time for the hedgewitch. The garden and nature have taken a battering from the winter storms, and new buds are pushing through the debris, which needs to be cleared. There are important festivals that need to be planned for: Ostara and Beltane. New life is everywhere, and elemental beings are waking from their winter sleep. As hedgewitches, we can feel this energy and this buzz, like the world is stretching and yawning.

Spring is a season in which all other seasons can be felt in one day. Sunshine, wind, hail, forgiving rainbows—this turbulent season is magical, and the weather can create imaginative outlets for the hedgewitch. The March snows can sweep across daffodil banks, leaving only their bright yellow heads peeping out among the white, cold blanket. The April gales and changeable weather can bring such wonderous delights as rainbows, blossoms, and, sadly, floods and devastation (as such, there is a prayer to the earth for healing from floods). May can bring sun so strong that a hedgewitch tending their garden can easily get burnt if they don't watch out!

There is something incredibly powerful at this transitional time of year: the vernal equinox. A time when the world is in balance, and an excellent time during which to cast several reaffirming spells to enhance all areas of life, from career, to love and relationships. As spring is a transitional time, it is also a time of hedge-riding and travelling to the other realm that beckons us.

NATURE'S BOUNTY: SPRING

Here is a list of all the good stuff that nature brings us in spring. Depending on where you live, many of these are readily available from the supermarket. Whenever you can, please try to buy or grow locally.

apples, asparagus, bay leaf, basil, beetroot, borage, broccoli, cabbage, carrots, cauliflower, celeriac, celery, chamomile, chard, chervil, chicory, chives, cress, elderflower, endive, fennel, garlic, garlic chives, Jerusalem artichoke, kale, lamb's lettuce, lavender, leeks, lemon balm, lettuce, lovage, mint, mushrooms, new potatoes, onions, oregano, parsley, parsnips, peas, pears, potatoes, radishes, red cabbage, rhubarb, rocket lettuce, rosemary, sage, shallots, sorrel, spinach, spring greens, spring onions, squash, strawberries, swede, tarragon, turnips, thyme, wood strawberries

From the Kitchen

The spring kitchen is a busy place, as the harvesting of fresh produce becomes important. The new herbs and blossoms only sprout once a year, and it's a perfect time to preserve these so that they can be used for the rest of the year. The jam and jelly recipes that follow feature blossoms and herbs that taste sweeter in the spring. The more you harvest herbs, the more they will grow back, so don't worry about picking new growth; it will return in abundance.

THE JAMS

The fruits of spring are often overlooked compared to the autumn fruits. However, spring fruits are just as delicious: rhubarb and apricots are just two varieties. Start making jam now; there is no need to wait until autumn to begin.

I always try to limit the amount of sugar; therefore, these recipes will not follow the traditional recipe for jam. Traditionally, all fruit jams followed this time-honoured code: one kilogram of sugar to one kilogram of fruit. But this is such a terribly high amount of sugar, and our lifestyles have changed; we must find healthier ways of making jams and marmalades. The reason for the traditional amount is that sugar was the key ingredient in preserving the fruit. Sugar, vinegar, and alcohol are all preservatives. Nevertheless, many of these recipes will have the sugar intake reduced considerably, and extra pectin will be added in the form of liquid pectin.

Always be careful when cooking jams as they can suddenly burn if you leave them too long. Make sure to watch the pan and keep stirring.

Rhubarb and Ginger Jam

Ingredients

900 grams / 2 pounds of trimmed rhubarb, thinly sliced

500 grams / 1 pound of jam sugar with added pectin

3 tablespoons of freshly chopped root ginger (optional—
some people don't like ginger)

½ bottle of liquid pectin

1 teaspoon of butter

A splash of cranberry juice

Method

Put fruit and sugar in a big, deep saucepan. Add a splash of water or cranberry juice—just enough so that the fruit and sugar won't burn. The fruit itself will begin to release its own juices quite quickly once it starts cooking, so don't put too much extra liquid in. Keep stirring until the sugar has dissolved. Bring to a boil and keep boiling for about ten to fifteen minutes. Stir occasionally to prevent burning.

If there is a foamy substance forming on the jam (it's called scum), add a teaspoon of butter to the boiling mixture and stir through.

Use the old method of testing jam. Have a saucer cooling in the fridge and place a teaspoon of the jam on it. Pop it back in the fridge for five minutes. If the jam has set, great; if it hasn't, pour the liquid pectin in and keep boiling for ten minutes, then retest with the saucer.

If you like the taste of fruit and there are still some larger pieces of undissolved rhubarb, keep the jam as it is. However, if you prefer a smoother jam, use a hand blender or potato masher while cooking.

Make sure you have at least four washed and sterilised jam jars ready. Keep them in a moderately heated oven for at least twenty minutes prior to ladling.

After the jam has reached its setting point, ladle it into the warmed, sterilised jars right to the top, then screw on the lids over waxed discs or cellophane tops secured with elastic bands. Decorate with a traditional material covering the top. Leave to cool, then label and date. Store in a cool place.

If the jam has not set, boil it again, stirring all the time to remove the excess liquid. The jam needs to be a thick, glossy consistency.

Rhubarb and Prosecco Jam

Ingredients

2 apples, washed and diced

2 pears, washed and diced

700 grams / 1.5 pounds of rhubarb, washed and sliced small

600 grams / 1.3 pounds of jam sugar with added pectin

¼ cup of prosecco

½ bottle of liquid pectin

1 teaspoon of butter

Splash of cherry juice

Method

Put all fruit, sugar, and a splash of cherry juice in a pan and bring to a boil. Follow the Rhubarb and Ginger Jam method. When the fruit is cooked, stir in prosecco, then allow to boil down. Test as normal with a saucer. If the jam sets easily, ladle into jars.

Spring Elderflower Jam
Ingredients
1 cup of elderflowers, washed
600 grams / 1.3 pounds of apricots
500 grams / 1 pound of strawberries
600 grams / 1.3 pounds of jam sugar with added pectin
½ bottle of liquid pectin
Splash of lemon juice

Method
Put fruit and flowers in a deep pan with sugar and a splash of lemon juice and slowly bring to a boil. Keep boiling for at least twenty minutes before following the recipe on Rhubarb and Ginger Jam. Saucer test, then ladle into jars when ready.

Hawthorn Hedgewitch Jam

Ingredients

500 grams/1 pound of apples
500 grams/1 pound of pears
1 cup of hawthorn flowers
600 grams/1.3 pounds of jam sugar with added pectin
Five star anises
1 lemon, sliced
2 limes, sliced

Method

Peel and quarter the apples and pears, removing the seeds and core, then finely dice. Rinse and drain the hawthorn flowers.

Put in a pan and bring to a boil, stirring constantly. Add the sliced lemon and limes. Cook for a good fifteen minutes. Do your saucer test for setting. If it sets, ladle into warm, sterilised jars. If not, boil down further, stirring all the time. Before you ladle, be sure to remove the star anises.

Spring Goddess Jam

Ingredients

1 cup of hawthorn flowers

1 cup of elderflowers

600 grams / 1.3 pounds of apricots, chopped

500 grams / 1 pound of pears, core removed, chopped

600 grams / 1.3 pounds of jam sugar with added pectin

½ bottle of liquid pectin

A generous splash of apricot liqueur (homemade if possible; see recipe in syrup section)

Method

Put the fruits into a large preserving pan with sugar and a generous splash of apricot liqueur. Bring to a boil. Cook over a low heat until fruit is soft, stirring gently. Gradually add the washed flowers and keep stirring. Allow to boil for at least fifteen minutes before usual procedure of testing and ladling into the sterilised jam jars.

THE JELLIES

Jellies are great accompaniments for cheeses and cold meats and are different from the usual chutneys and sandwich spreads. Try a jelly for a sandwich or salad—they are packed full of spring energy.

Remember, herbs grow better when they have been picked and used. If herbs are not used, they go to flower and lose their taste. Therefore, pick as many herbs as you can, and don't worry about leaving the plant almost bare—mints, lemon balm, sages, and many herbs relish a good plucking!

Experiment with herbs and flavours for your jellies, but follow this standard recipe for Thyme Jelly. Moreover, jellies require gelatine to solidify, and there are plenty of vegetarian substitutes out there. The seaweed variety is particularly good.

Thyme Jelly

Ingredients

500 millilitres / 2 cups of water

30 grams / 2 ounces of powdered gelatine or 1 packet of gelatine

500 grams / 1 pound of demerara sugar

250 millilitres / 1 cup of white vinegar

30 grams / 2 ounces of thyme, washed and chopped
(use different varieties of thyme if possible)

Method

Boil water and sugar for ten minutes, then reduce heat and stir in the gelatine. Simmer until dissolved.

Stir in vinegar and thyme and simmer for ten more minutes. Remove from heat and steep for a good twenty minutes; the longer the better. After straining, transfer jelly to warm, sterilised jars, exactly like the jam jars, then seal just as you would with jam.

Chives and Parsley Jelly

Ingredients

500 millilitres / 2 cups of water

30 grams / 2 ounces of powdered gelatine or 1 packet of
gelatine

250 millilitres / 1 cup of white wine vinegar

30 grams / 8 ounces of chives, washed and chopped

30 grams / 8 ounces of parsley, washed and chopped

250 grams / ½ pound of demerara sugar

Method

Use the same method as with the Thyme Jelly. Remember, the longer you let it steep, the stronger the taste will be.

Fennel and Sorrel Jelly

Ingredients

1 cup of fennel, washed thoroughly

¼ cup of sorrel leaves

500 millilitres / 2 cups of water

30 grams / 2 ounces of powdered gelatine or 1 packet of gelatine

250 millilitres / 1 cup of white wine vinegar

250 grams / ½ pound of demerara sugar

Method

Follow the same method for Thyme Jelly. Remember, the longer you leave the herbs to steep, the stronger the flavour.

Spring Dandelion Jelly

This is a sweet jelly with the flavour and consistency of honey. Furthermore, dandelions are high in antioxidants, such as vitamin C and luteolin, which reduce free radicals (major cancer-causing agents) in the body, thereby reducing the risk of cancer.[4]

Ingredients

4 cups of dandelion flowers (no base or stem, just the flowers), washed

600 millilitres/2.5 cups of water

30 grams/2 ounces of gelatine or 1 packet of gelatine

2 tablespoons of lemon juice

300 grams/0.6 pound of sugar

Method

Put flowers and water in a preserving pan or a deep saucepan. Boil for about ten minutes before removing from heat. Allow to steep for at least an hour. The longer it steeps, the deeper the colour.

Line a colander with a paper towel and strain the mixture. Place the liquid back in the pan. Add the gelatine, sugar, and lemon juice and bring it to a boil again. Stir con-

----

4. Ansley Hill, "13 Potential Health Benefits of Dandelion," *Healthline*, July 18, 2018, https://www.healthline.com/nutrition/dandelion-benefits.

stantly, making sure all the sugar dissolves (follow gelatine instructions).

Boil the mixture for about ten minutes before pouring it into sterilised jars. Leave to cool before labelling and dating.

If any of the jellies have not set after two hours, boil again and add thirty grams of gelatine to the mixture. Don't forget to sterilise the jars again.

THE SPRING RENEWALS: TONICS AND TEAS

Spring is such a powerful season, and the flowers and plants that grow at this time are gifts from nature. These powerful plants pack such a punch to our internal systems that they are a wake-up call to our bodies.

Our sluggish winter digestive systems are given a kick with these ingredients—not discussing them would be a crime against nature and the Goddess herself. Plants grow as and when needed, and it's amazing that the earth bursts from its winter slumber with vitality-boosting flowers, herbs, and so on.

Certain foods—such as watercress, dandelions, nettles, cabbage, and leeks, to name but a few—can renew our energy and rid the body of toxins accumulated throughout the long winter months of possible overeating and indulgence.

Spring is a time of new life and regeneration, so let's use this season's power and resources to renew ourselves.

Spring Tonic

Ingredients

250 millilitres / 1 cup of carrot juice
125 millilitres / ½ cup of celery juice
1 garlic clove
½ cup of fresh parsley (plus a few sprigs to garnish)

Method

Blend all the ingredients together in a liquidizer or blender. Serve with a garnish of parsley. Drink immediately.

This rather thick juice is a perfect cleanser as all the ingredients aid in the elimination of toxins via the kidneys. When detoxing, always drink plenty of good, clean water.

Beetroot and Carrot Cleanser
Ingredients

3 large carrots, washed

2 medium beetroots, washed

Fresh coriander leaves to garnish, chopped

Method

Put all the vegetables through a juicer. Garnish with the coriander. Drink immediately.

This is a great drink to stimulate the liver and bowel functions as it enhances the elimination of toxins and wastes, making it a perfect remedy for constipation. If you are suffering with constipation, drink this before you go to bed, then have hot lemon water first thing when you get up in the morning.

Carrot and Rosemary Juice
Ingredients

125 millilitres / ½ cup of carrot juice

125 millilitres / ½ cup of celery juice

3 soft sprigs of fresh rosemary (or strip the leaves from
the stalk)

Freshly ground pepper (optional)

Method

Blend the carrot and celery juices and rosemary together
in a blender. Season with pepper (though this is optional)
and drink immediately.

Although a great cleansing drink for the spring, this is
also good for those who suffer with migraines, so much
so that Grandma advised drinking a cup of this regularly
as a preventative medicine for the dreaded headaches.

Dandelion Beer

Ingredients

250 grams / 1 cup of dandelion plants (young plants taste
sweeter)

8 pints / 1 gallon of water

30 grams / 2 ounces of root ginger, sliced

500 grams / 1 pound of demerara sugar

1 lemon (include finely peeled rind and its juice)

25 grams/0.8 ounce of cream of tartar
7 grams/1 tablespoon of dried brewer's yeast or 1 packet
   of brewer's yeast

Method
Remove all the fibrous roots on the young dandelion plants and leave just the main root. Place in a large saucepan with the water, ginger, and lemon rind and bring to a boil. Simmer for ten minutes. After, strain and pour onto the sugar and cream of tartar in a fermentation bucket. Stir until the sugar has dissolved.

Start the yeast, following the packet's instructions, and then add it to the mixture with the lemon juice. Stir, then cover and leave in a warm room for three days. After, strain into screw top bottles. It will be ready to drink after one week, and kept in a cool place, it will last about a month. That's if you don't drink it all.

Hedgewitch Decongestant
At this time of year, the dreaded spring colds and flu viruses attack, and sinus infections are all around as the weather

changes its mind on an hourly basis. This old remedy is just right for relieving the symptoms of colds and flu along with fevers, catarrh, and sinus congestion.

Ingredients
2 teaspoons of fresh elderflowers
2 teaspoons of fresh lime flowers
2 teaspoons of fresh peppermint leaves
2 teaspoons of fresh yarrow
1 pint of boiling water
Honey to taste

Method
Place the herbs in a teapot and pour the boiling water over them. Leave to infuse for ten to fifteen minutes, then sweeten with honey if you like. Drink a hot cupful three to five times a day or until the congestion clears.

THE TEAS

Although tea is an actual plant grown predominantly in India and China, many people have made "teas" from different herbs, leaves, and plants. These herbal teas are technically infusions. The boiling water is poured over the leaves and allowed to steep for at least five minutes, then poured into a cup to enjoy. Sugar and honey or a range of other spices and fruits can be added to sweeten the tea if so desired.

Teas are incredibly versatile. They can be cold or hot, frozen and used as an ice cube in a summer fruit punch, or made into an alcoholic beverage or a celebratory drink.

Here is a selection of spring teas, all excellent for renewal and rejuvenation. Remember, these recipes are just ideas, and you can experiment with your own flavours. Enjoy.

Magical Basil Tea
Ingredients
1 tablespoon of fresh basil leaves
1 tablespoon of fresh lemon balm leaves
1 pint of boiling water

Method
Place washed herbs in a teapot and pour boiling water over them. Cover and leave to infuse for about ten to fifteen minutes. Then drink, adding desired sweeteners.

Magical basil water is perfect for easing stress, including headaches, tension pains, and migraines.

Lettuce Tea
Ingredients
3 or 4 lettuce leaves

½ pint of water

A couple of sprigs of fresh mint

Method
Simmer the lettuce leaves in water in a covered pan for fifteen minutes. Then remove from the heat, adding the mint. Leave to steep for about five to ten minutes. Strain and drink.

This was an old English cure for insomnia, so have a cup before you go to bed if you have trouble sleeping.

Chamomile and Catmint Tea
Ingredients
1 teaspoon of fresh chamomile flowers

2 teaspoons of fresh catmint

1 pint of water

Method

Place herbs in a teapot and pour boiling water over them. Leave for ten to fifteen minutes to infuse, and then drink.

This is a great tea if you are suffering from the spasm stages of irritable bowel syndrome. It relieves a tense stomach.

Elderflower and Peppermint Tea

Ingredients

2 teaspoons of fresh elderflowers
2 teaspoons of fresh peppermint leaves
1 pint of water

Method

Place the herbs in a teapot and pour boiling water over them. Allow to steep for ten to fifteen minutes. Drink as much as you want and sweeten with honey if desired.

This is a perfect tea when suffering from the dreaded seasonal flu.

THE SYRUPS

Spring is a wonderful time of renewal and regeneration. As we have seen in previous sections, plants and foods are given to us from nature for our benefit. Therefore, here in this section, there are five recipes for syrups using ingredients that are detoxing, cleansing, and purifying.

The Goddess has it already worked out for us, and all we need to do is introduce the changing seasons into our diets: eat the fruits and vegetables that our country supplies naturally so that we can be well all season. And there is no better way to find out what grows naturally than a day out of the city and hedge-riding through the countryside. Take advantage and go grocery shopping where everything is free. (However, don't collect anything that may have pesticides and all the other nasty sprays we lather on nature.)

In this section, we are going to make syrups (plus some alcoholic types) that are of benefit to us—medicinally, of course! They can be a bit finicky, but they are worth the effort and make great presents.

Thyme Syrup

Use any variety of thyme. Lemon thyme has a unique flavour and is quite good for clearing coughs.

Ingredients

50 grams / 3 ounces of fresh thyme, washed
1 pint / 2.5 cups of boiling water
300 grams / 0.6 pound of runny honey
150 grams / 0.3 pound of sugar

Method

Boil the water in a deep saucepan and add thyme. Leave to infuse for ten to fifteen minutes—the longer the better. Sieve the mixture, removing any larger leaves of thyme. Keep some smaller leaves in. Heat up to a simmer, adding the sugar and honey. Stir the mixture as it starts to thicken and skim off any scum. Leave to cool, then pour into a glass bottle and store in the refrigerator.

You can use this like a cough syrup and take two teaspoons three times a day for coughs and colds.

Tudor Rosemary and Lemon Syrup

Ingredients

2 cups of rosemary sprigs, washed and stripped from
   the stem
500 grams/1 pound of demerara or brown sugar
1 pint/2.5 cups of water
1 lemon, juiced

Method

Bring rosemary and water to a boiling point in a deep saucepan. Boil for about ten to fifteen minutes, then leave to infuse for a good twenty minutes or longer. Strain and return to the pan, adding the lemon juice and sugar. Heat slowly, stirring all the time until the sugar is dissolved. Boil briskly for about five minutes or until the syrup starts to thicken. Remove from heat and allow to cool before pouring into sterilised jars or glass bottles. Seal with air-tight lids when completely cooled.

This is a great cure for hangovers. Make a batch of it when having a party or celebrations such as May Day or Ostara. If you have friends staying over and hangovers are around the morning after, administer one to two table-spoons until the hangover subsides.

Cabbage and Coriander Syrup

This may sound absolutely disgusting, but on a chilly spring day when your sinuses are all bunged up, this syrup can help—plus making it really channels your inner witch.

Ingredients
2 teaspoons of coriander seeds
1 white cabbage, finely chopped and washed
1 jar of runny honey

Method
Crush coriander seeds using a pestle and mortar, releasing their goodness. Put them in a large bowl with the chopped cabbage. Pour in the honey, making sure the cabbage leaves are covered. Press down the leaves if they're not. Cover the bowl with a clean tea towel and leave overnight. After, strain the syrup through a sieve and bottle it up in a glass bottle. Take two teaspoons three times a day

until sinuses improve. This syrup is good as a preventative during hay fever time!

Nettle Beer

Ingredients

500 grams / 1 pound of nettle tips
1 lemon, juiced (include peeled rind)
4 pints / 9.5 cups of water
250 grams / ½ pound of demerara sugar
15 grams / 2 tablespoons / 1 packet of cream of tartar
7.5 grams / 1 tablespoon / 1 packet of brewer's yeast

Method

Place nettle tips, lemon rind, and water in a large saucepan. Bring to a boil. Reduce the heat and simmer for about thirty minutes. Strain onto the sugar and cream of tartar in a fermentation bucket and stir well. Follow the yeast instructions and start it off, then add it and the lemon juice to the cooled mixture in the bucket. Cover and leave in a room for three days.

After, strain the nettle beer into strong bottles, but don't tighten up, as the mixture is still quite gassy. Leave for a week to settle before drinking. You can serve it cooled or with ice.

Apricot Liqueur
Ingredients
4 kilos/8.5 pounds of ripe apricots, washed, quartered, and kernels removed
680 grams/1.5 pounds of sugar
½ litre/2 cups of water

Method
Place water and sugar in a deep saucepan and bring to a boiling point, stirring all the time. Reduce heat and simmer for a couple of minutes as you skim off the foam. Remove from the heat and let the sugar syrup cool to room temperature.

After, put apricot quarters in a glass container and pour the cooled syrup over them. Tie the neck of the container with cheesecloth or muslin and leave in a dark place for four days to ferment.

Check on the mixture. There should be foam on the surface, a hissing sound, and an acidic odour. Cover with an airtight lid and leave the mixture for forty days to ferment. The exact time depends on the sugar content of the apricots used. When fermentation is over, there should be no hissing sound or foam on top of the mixture.

Filter the apricot through a few layers of cheesecloth or muslin. Squeeze the pulp and add the liquid to the alcohol. Bottle the liqueur and leave it for about one month in a fridge or cellar.

From the Cauldron

In the spring, nature is bursting all around us, and the Goddess leaves many presents for us in the shape of flowers and warmer weather. There are a number of spring festivals that embrace this change, as the desire to practice outside is overwhelming, especially for this hedgewitch—I prefer to be outside even on a cold, rainy spring day!

SPRING CRAFTS

The seasonal crafts of spring focus around our festivals and things we can make to celebrate. We are bringing nature indoors for celebrations, though one would hope that by the time Beltane comes around in May (in the northern hemisphere), we can be outdoors, enjoying a rain-free day of sunshine and flowers.

The crafts we can make this time of year are ones of flowers and table decorations for Ostara, Beltane, and the vernal equinox. Although many combine the equinox with Ostara, astronomically speaking, they can occur on different days, so it is best to check from year to year. There is also Hexennacht, the night before Beltane, which is a festival celebration and one you may choose to celebrate individually.

Hexennacht, or Witches' Night, happens every April 30, and the celebrations continue into May 1, which is May Day and Beltane. Hexennacht is also called Walpurgis Night, the feast of Saint Walpurgis. Its origins are steeped in Celtic traditions, and it is often referred to as the Spring Halloween.

As always, try to get outside as much as you can, gathering anything and everything from nature.

March Storms Wand
You Will Need
A twig from a tree of your choosing (or from one that
    has chosen you!)
A selection of ribbons and crystals
Craft wire
Pliers
A knife (or athame, a ritual knife)
Magical salt
A hot glue gun
Imagination

After the gales and winds of March, you may suddenly start to see twigs that are perfect for a wand. You might be walking through a park and see a strong twig that you feel you must pick up. You might even be walking a city street on the way to work, see a twig, and just know that you are meant to pick it up and take it home with you. Do so. This is the Craft saying you need a wand. Please do not purposely go into a city park and start hurting trees. We work with nature. We are protectors of nature. Some may say, "Well, I asked the tree for it," but that still does not make it right.

Suppose you have now found a twig or stick; what do you do to turn it into a wand? The stick needs to be about twelve inches or thirty centimetres in length.

Now, wands, like almost everything in the Craft, are subjective. What you do is entirely up to you. Some people strip the bark off the stick, others keep it on and work with nature. If you do want yours stripped, use your athame to whittle the bark off (always cutting away from you). All you are doing is peeling back the bark to expose the clean wood underneath.

Further, it is up to you how you want to decorate it. Before you go to sleep, ask to see your finished wand in a dream. You should dream about it then, and you will know. If you see crystals and gemstones on it, then buy some. To make it easier, you can buy gemstones with holes already drilled through them; these are much easier to attach to your wand with craft wire.

To attach your crystals, slowly wind the craft wire around your wand. Add a crystal here and there as you go. Once finished, wind the wire around and snip it off with the pliers. If you want a large gemstone at the top of your wand, secure this one in place with a small amount of glue. If you do not want to attach your gemstones with the wire, you can always glue them into place. You could have large hunks all together in different formations for different effects, but make sure they work together in harmony.

Ribbons are also good for decorating your wand, and you could use the correspondences if there is something you want to work for, such as money, love, or a career. After you have your wire secured, add the ribbon, wrapping it around and gluing it into place at the bottom of your wand so this acts as a grip. After you have attached all the ribbons and crystals with the glue, leave your wand to dry. Then you need to cleanse it. You can use your magic salt for this. I suggest using sun salt, as you want the wand to be purified with the powers of pure light energy and strength. All you do with this salt is sprinkle it over your wand, imagining the sun's rays infusing it with power after saying, "Blessed be, so mote it be."

Ostara Centrepiece
You Will Need
Used, washed eggshells
Soya candle wax
Small candlewicks, waxed
Candle wax colours or wax crayons

An Ostara centrepiece is exactly what you would imagine it to be: eggs and flowers. However, make something a little different. In used, carefully washed eggshells, create candles. Place a small wick inside the half-cracked eggshell and pour candle wax in; a little will go a long way. Make them in beautiful pastel colours of pinks, blues, and yellows, which are perfect for spring. Place the eggs around the centrepiece, which could be a tray covered in fresh flowers such as daffodils, forget-me-nots, tulips, and bluebells, or whatever flowers are in season where you live.

You could also create miniature besoms using the same technique as the larger broom and place them around the tray with ribbons and other gifts from nature.

April Hexennacht Broom

Hexennacht, or Witches' Night, occurs the night before Beltane, one of the most powerful festivals of the witches' year. It is the fire festival and a time when the Goddess has returned completely. Bonfires are lit, and great rejoicing occurs as we welcome the Goddess of the spring and summer back into the world.

You Will Need
Twigs about 40 to 50 centimetres/1 foot in length
Broom handle 4 to 5 feet long
Collection of ribbons, crystals, ivy, or anything you like
Ball of twine

Despite what you think, making your own broom is actually easy. Decide if you are going to use traditional twigs. If so, get out in nature and collect twigs about forty to fifty centimetres in length. The winter storms have bashed the trees all season, so there should be plenty to pick up from the forest floor. Take a bag with you and spend the day foraging in the forest, wood, or even city park for twigs. You can buy a broom handle, but once again, it's even better if nature delivers a perfect branch about four to five feet long.

When you get home, sort out your bounty and begin the process of wrapping the twigs around one end of the branch or pole. Tie and bind with twine tightly. Add ribbons, real ivy, crystals, and all manner of objects that are relevant and personal to you. This is your broomstick. It has your energy and your magic installed in it with every twig attached.

Leave it in the moonlight to be infused with the Goddess's power on the night of a full moon. After it is charged, use it as you would a normal broom, but keep it for Hexennacht as part of your celebrations.

Rainbow Mobile

You Will Need

1 twig about 40 to 50 centimetres / 1 foot long

Ribbons or twine

Hot glue gun

Selection of flowers, shells, and/or sea glass (pieces of
  nature that represent the rainbow)

This is a challenging craft task—not challenging to make, but challenging to come up with. Each year, try to make a mobile that represents each colour of the rainbow: red, orange, yellow, blue, green, indigo, and violet.

It is easy to make a dried flower mobile, so I challenge myself to make something out of shells, sea glass washed from the winter's stormy seas, bright pebbles, stones, branches, or feathers. Though I must confess, the bluebell does make an appearance each year on the rainbow mobile, only because it represents the fae in all their innocence.

To make the mobile, find a good-size twig and simply attach your rainbow objects with natural twine ... or cheat with the corresponding coloured ribbon.

May Day Bath Bomb

You Will Need

5 ounces / ½ cup of powdered citric acid

8 ounces / 1 cup of soda bicarbonate

6 ounces / ¾ cup of Epsom salts

Selection of food dyes

Selection of dried or fresh flowers

Bath bomb moulds

A little water

Essential oils (optional)

Method

In a large bowl, mix powdered citric acid with soda bicarbonate and Epsom salts. Make sure all ingredients are mixed well together. Add a little bit of water (a spray bottle makes it easier). Just a few sprays of water, as too much will cause the mixture to dissolve, and you will have to start from scratch. The water is just to bind the mixture together before you add your colourings, essential oils, and flowers.

The colours ideal for May are yellow, orange, and red. Remember, Beltane is a fire festival. The essential oils can be lily of the valley, lilac, honeysuckle, and even bluebell. Mix well together, then press firmly into rounded moulds: a dome mould is perfect. Make sure to press hard, as the mixture needs to be compact in the mould to reduce cracking.

Let them dry for four hours at least. If they are still damp after this time, take them out of the moulds and let the air do its work. After they have thoroughly dried, store the bath bombs in an airtight container. Do not allow them to get wet or else they will dissolve. Just pop one into your bath, relax, and allow yourself to be cleansed in a May Day bath bomb. You could always put hawthorn flowers in the mixture to add that extra May spring feeling.

Experiment with mould shapes and essential oils. As this is spring and we often get colds and the general sniffles, make a eucalyptus and rosemary oil bath fizzy to help you breathe better. There are so many possibilities with these, and they make great gifts.

SPRING SPELLS

This is the season of flash floods, and as such, there is a spell for those affected by this devastating weather phenomenon. The other spells in this section are all spells that can be harnessed by the festival and the changing time of the year. Although these spells can be performed at other times of the year, they are particularly potent during spring. Activating charms and enchantments are particularly strong in March, while performing a desire spell during the week of Beltane is especially powerful, as this is the festival of sex, fertility, Mars, fire, and passion.

Lucky Charms of March

March is magical. Not only is it the first official month of spring, but it is the month that witnesses the vernal equinox, which is a deeply magical time. Activating charms during this powerful time gives the object extra oomph. The types of charms are countless. Here is a list of just some lucky charms people have used, and still use, to ward off evil and stay clear of hexes and curses.

- Egyptian scarabs
- St. Christopher medals
- Four-leaf clovers
- Letters of protection (carried by soldiers, for example)
- Human hair (very popular in Victorian England!)
- Lucky coins
- The cone from a hemlock tree, which is viewed as a fertility charm (though I have a cone from a cedar of Lebanon tree as a protection for the house)

Lucky charm bracelets are often worn today by people who are unaware of their magical associations. A charm basically means a chant or incantation recited to produce some good or bad magical effect (the term *charm* means to sing). An object may be charmed in this manner, or the charm may be written down. When worn or carried, these charmed objects are called amulets.

When you first get your charm, you need to cleanse and charge it. You can cleanse it under running water, so hold it under the tap for a few minutes, or pass it through smoke from incense. Leave it in the sun or moonlight to charge for a few hours. After, hold it in your hands and concentrate upon it. Imagine all the things you want it to do. Imagine a good life with your charm, or your charmed life of good.

While still holding the charm in your hands, say,

> *I dedicate this charm of mine to the highest good*
> *of all who come in contact with it.*

Charming a Piece of Jewellery

Find a piece of jewellery that you like to wear and use regularly. It could even be a watch.

Hold the jewellery in your hands and say,

> *Bless this [jewellery].*
> *Charm it well.*
> *Good luck to the wearer forevermore.*

Good luck spread to me every day in every way.
An' it harm none, so mote it be.

Equinox Transitional Meditation

The word *equinox* comes from the Latin words *aequus*, which means equal, and *nox*, which means night. On the March equinox, the sun crosses the celestial equator.

Equinoxes are the only two times a year that the sun rises due east and sets due west for all of us on Earth! Use this energy to project yourself through meditation to another realm.

Lighting a yellow candle, waft the light around you. Have a mirror nearby so that you can see your reflection. Say,

Light and dark, day and night,
grant me safe passage in both dark and light.
Journey I must, both day and night,
to realms both dark and light.
Send me now, journey bound,
as I venture from this ground.

Watch the candle flicker in the dark and let go of all worries, stresses, and cares of the day. Take several deep breaths and let go. Let your mind wonder, look through the mirror, and watch as images appear.

April Flash Floods Spell

If there has been a flood, cast a healing spell for those involved. Call out to the Goddess and the earth to help and heal.

Light a blue candle and draw a circle in salt on a tray while saying,

> *The waters have risen and the earth doth drown.*
> *Stop the flood from deep within the ground.*
> *Earth, call out to your roots,*
> *"Drink up the flood, you thirsty roots."*

Keep the candle burning as long as possible, but never keep a candle burning unattended.

Beltane Passion Spell

If you want a year of passion and sex, perform this spell at Beltane. On the night of Beltane, stand naked in front of a mirror and say into your reflection,

> *From Beltane night to the next,*
> *commence a year of sex.*
> *Let the fire of this night rise within me.*
> *Flames of passion burn within,*
> *releasing my power therein.*
> *With this body, I create desire.*
> *To all who see me with passion fire.*

If you are with a partner, perfect. Have a wonderful year. If not, be careful, and always practice safe sex.

SPRING ELEMENTALS

The spring elementals that we can encounter during these three months of March, April, and May are as varied as they are marvellous. Although the elemental kingdom is always around us, even in winter, the spring is when things really start to heat up and we suddenly become aware that the wee folk are about.

Elves

In Iceland, the belief in elves is so strong that there is a special school to learn about them. The school is called Alfaskolinn, and it is based in Reykjavik, the capitol. It teaches students about the hidden people and the thirteen different types of elves.[5] In Iceland, there are even special "elf investigators" who make sure that potential new buildings will not disturb the elves; there are plenty of tales about jinxed buildings and cursed factories and homes because people ignored the warnings and disturbed the elves.

Elves and dwarves feature in many cultures all over the world. The little people have walked Earth as long as we have been here. In Central America, there is the legend of the Red Dwarf, who uses his axe to cause sparks so that a seer can interpret someone's fortune from them. In

5. The school's information can be found at https://theelfschool.com/.

Native American cultures, the dwarves and elves appear in many myths and legends, usually associated with mountains and rivers, such as the Awakkule, who are strong, mountain-dwelling dwarves.

Elves are distinct from other beings of spirit as they do not have wings and are very humanoid in appearance. They often are very ethereal, with blond hair and blue eyes. They like a good singsong. Elves are known for their dances and can be seen dancing over meadows at night and on misty mornings. They leave behind "fairy rings," which are circles of mushrooms or bare patches of soil.

Elf Connection

If you would like to connect with the elves in your garden or forest, say this spell three times and watch how the nature around you begins to respond. Things to look out for are the feelings of cobwebs across your face or of serenity flowing over you, or a deep stillness rushing throughout your immediate environment. The birds may even stop singing. These are all indicators of elemental contact.

I call upon the elfin sprite.
Come to me both day and night.

The Leprechaun

It was in the eighth century that leprechauns made their first appearance in Ireland, living in the hills and mountains in a secret, sacred, enchanted world that only they could find through the use of their shillelaghs. The shillelagh is a short, thick club that was carried as a defence against muggers and thieves. It is also known as a cudgel and is still popular with people today for the same purpose. Many depictions of leprechauns show them with their shillelaghs, and given that this was a weapon, one can deduce that a leprechaun would defend himself at any cost.

As leprechauns are fabulous makers of shoes, you could connect with them by sorting out all your shoes. Light a green candle, put on your favourite music, and sort out all your shoes and boots. Clean and polish them and give away those you have not worn for years. If there are shoes that need mending, have them repaired.

Leprechaun Connection

If you have Wellington boots or shoes that are no longer worth wearing as they cannot be repaired, you could make them into plant pots. Spray them gold and put a trailing lobelia in them; this comes in a range of colours and is a lovely bedding plant for the summer that the elementals will appreciate. Leprechauns are spirit elementals with dominion over the earth, and that includes the plants and flowers. Ferns, lilies, and flowers of golden yellow are the best ones to represent the wee folk of Ireland in your garden.

The Lady of the Lake

The Lady of the Lake first makes an appearance in the legends and stories of King Arthur and Excalibur. This mysterious lady holds the sword Excalibur as the symbol of eternal power, magic, and nobility. Hers is the watery world of magic and mystery. Just as the Lady of the Lake was the guardian of Excalibur, she was also revered as a Celtic goddess in some tales. However, the Lady of the Lake is regarded as one of the Ancient Ones: ageless and beautiful and immune to the effects of disease, the Ancient Ones are beings who have been here long before humans and are the keepers of ancient knowledge. They are neither angels, nor fairies, nor gods.

Lady of the Lake Connection

The Lady of the Lake is an ancient wisdom keeper of spirit. The information she knows and understands is unimaginable. She can be called upon by having a piece of aquamarine in your pocket, or a piece of aqua aura. These stones are beautiful and immensely powerful: a connection to the Lady and a reminder that the Ancient Ones are always with us. Fill an obsidian bowl or black-bottomed bowl with water at a full moon and charge the crystals in it. If possible, place the bowl in view of the moon's rays, saying these words:

Lady of the Lake, I call to thee,
help me in my endeavours.
Let these stones serve me well the whole month long,

help me see the right from the wrong.
Lady of the Lake, always be with me.
An' it harm none, so mote it be.

In the morning, take the stones out of the bowl and leave them to dry naturally. Throw the water away, giving thanks for its healing, cleansing energies. With every use of your bowl, always tip the water away so that the bowl is dry for most of the time; it should only have water in it when you wish to use it for a ritual or for cleansing crystals.

SPRING ESBAT RITUAL

The spring Esbat ritual is one of renewal. We also give thanks for the passing winter as we focus our intent and wishes for the coming spring and summer.

On the first night of any spring full moon, ask the universe to grant your desires of renewal and regeneration in all your projects and, especially, health.

If you can perform the Esbat outside, raise your hands toward the moon and say,

Welcome spring with zeal and zest.
Thank you for the winter's rest.
My health, renew and rejuvenate,
with spring power to invigorate.
All I can be and seek.
My new strength and energy will meet.
Abound anew within me now.
Blessed spring moon, please endow.

After, meditate awhile on all the projects you would like to do for spring. Think about how you would like to change and work that into your daily life.

SPRING SEASONAL CORRESPONDENCE CHART

Here are additional spring correspondences we can use:

Colours: Pastel blues, pinks, yellows, creams

Crystals: Rainbow quartz, rainbow pyrite

Flowers: Bluebells, campanula, daffodils, tulips, daisies

Incense: Sage, eucalyptus, lemon

Oils: Orange, vanilla, magnolia

Weather: Rainbows, showers, wind

Deities: Manannan, Ostara, Brigid, Flora

Elementals: Fae, leprechauns, sprites

Planets: Mars, Venus, Jupiter

Numbers: 3, 7, 9

Summer

In the summer, we find two important festivals: Midsummer and Lammas. The June Midsummer celebrations come with an explosion of flowers and colours, providing a treasure trove of craft activities for the industrious hedge-witch to complete, from pressing and drying flowers, to making bath salts and flower essences—not to mention all the art that can be made with both leaves and flowers.

The July searing sun can often make the gardens feel dry, and we are busy caring for nature, using water from barrels. This month, we often perform a rain spell, but we need to monitor it and be careful, as weather spells, once made, cannot be put back in the jar, as it were. During this time, you will discover ancient ribbon magic and the notorious nine-knot spell in its original form.

In the northern hemisphere, August brings a turning point: the festival of Lammas. This festival is a rather depressing one, as it signifies the loss of summer and the coming autumn. It is regarded as the first festival of the harvest when the first fruits arrive, and the Lammas bread becomes a gift to the gods as gratitude for the coming harvest.

In this season, flowers are in full bloom, and herbs, especially lavender, are particularly potent. However, although a wonderful and majestic herb, there are those who are allergic to lavender; therefore, all recipes and crafts can be made with an alternative of either rose petals or violets. These three summer flowers are interchangeable: lavender, roses, and violets.

NATURE'S BOUNTY: SUMMER

The fruits most prevalent in summer are strawberries, raspberries, nectarines, plums, and loganberries, to name but a few. Depending on where you live, these are readily available in the supermarket's frozen section. This list gives an idea of fruits and vegetables that are plentiful during summer. All are interchangeable. For example, a substitute for loganberries can be blueberries.

apples, angelica, asparagus, bay leaf, basil, beans, beetroot, blackberries, black currants, blueberries, borage, broccoli, cabbage, carrots, cauliflower, celeriac, celery, chamomile, chard, chervil, cherries, chicory, chives, courgettes, cress, cucumber, dill, eggplants, fennel, figs, garlic, garlic chives, globe artichoke, gooseberries, grapes, hyssop, kohl rabi, lettuce, lavender, lemon balm, loganberries, lovage, marjoram, marrows, medlar, melon, mint, mushrooms, nectarines, onions, oregano, parsley, peas, pears, peppers, peaches, plums, potatoes, raspberries, red cabbage, red currants, rhubarb, rocket lettuce, rosemary, runner beans, sage, shallots, sorrel, spinach, spring onions, strawberries, sweetcorn, tarragon, thyme, tomatoes, turnips, wood strawberries

EDIBLE FLOWERS

Here is a list of edible flowers so you can experiment with jellies and other edible projects. All are interchangeable and can be substituted for one another depending on which is readily available in your country. Similarly, the projects for lavender can be changed for any of these flowers.

lilac, peony, sunflower, dahlia, pansy, lavender, elderflower, marigold, hibiscus, chrysanthemum, dandelion, snapdragon, violets, rose, nasturtium, apple blossom, chive blossom, carnations, dianthus, bachelor's buttons, squash blossoms

From the Kitchen

The emphasis of the summer kitchen for me is trying to harvest as many of the beautiful, edible flowers available at this time as possible. The jam, jelly, chutney, and odd marmalade recipes are infused with flowers. The one herb that is prevalent throughout the summer in my garden is lavender, so please excuse my indulgence of recipes that add this delightful plant. Remember, all the edible flowers from the list are interchangeable and can be substituted for one another.

THE JAMS

The fruits of summer are a blessing and are not to be wasted whatsoever. Use as much of them as you can. Make sure to save jam and other mason jars all year, as nature's bounty soon comes around with its gracious fruit basket.

Strawberry Jam
Ingredients
500 grams/1 pound of strawberries
500 grams/1 pound of preserving sugar
2 tablespoons of pectin powder/half a bottle of liquid
    pectin
Fresh lemon juice (optional)
1 teaspoon of butter

Method
Wash and clean the strawberries, remove all stalks, and put them in a deep saucepan with the preserving sugar.

Cook on a moderate heat and gently bring to a boil. Stir occasionally, and make sure to skim off the scum that forms at the top. Boil gently until the jam sets when tested on a cold plate. You could add some freshly squeezed lemon juice, as this helps draw out the natural pectin of the fruit. Add a teaspoon of butter to the boiling mixture and stir through.

Use the old method of testing jam. Have a saucer cooling in the fridge and place a teaspoon of jam on it. Pop it back in the fridge for five minutes. If the jam hasn't set, pour the liquid pectin in and keep boiling for ten minutes. Retest with the saucer.

If you like the taste of fruit and there are still some larger pieces of undissolved strawberry, keep the consistency of the jam as it is. However, if you prefer a smoother jam, blast it with a hand blender or potato masher while cooking.

After the jam has reached its setting point, ladle it into warm, sterilised jars right to the top, then screw on lids over waxed discs or cellophane tops secured with elastic bands.

Decorate with a traditional material covering the top. Leave to cool, then label and date. Store in a cool place.

Blueberry and Lavender Jam

Ingredients
680 grams / 1.5 pounds of fresh or frozen blueberries
500 grams / 1 pound of jam or preserving sugar
2 tablespoons of honey
½ lemon, zested and juiced
1 tablespoon of fresh lavender buds or flowers
½ bottle of liquid pectin
1 teaspoon of butter

Method
Grind the lavender buds with a pestle and mortar and leave them to one side. Add all the other ingredients (except the liquid pectin) into a deep saucepan and bring to a boil, stirring all the time. Cook for about fifteen minutes, then add the crushed lavender and stir well. Lower to a medium heat and cook for ten minutes before trying the cold saucer test. If the jam sets after five minutes in the fridge, ladle it into a jar. If not, add the liquid pectin.

Cook for ten minutes. Test once more, then ladle into sterilised jam jars. If the jam is still not setting, boil again and keep stirring to reduce the liquid.

Rose Petal Jam

This is a wonderful, magical recipe and great to make with children, as the rose petals lose their colour while cooking, and when the lemon juice is added—*voilà!* The colour magically reappears, brighter than before.

Always try to pick wild rose petals and make sure they have not been contaminated with insecticide. Thoroughly wash before using. My great-grandmother always sprinkled a little salt in the water and left the rose petals soaking for about an hour before rinsing well and using, but it is entirely up to you. But please wash them, as creepy crawlies may have found their home in them.

Ingredients
2 cups of rose petals
2 pints of water
1 lemon, zested and juiced

1 cup of jam sugar with added pectin
½ bottle of liquid pectin

Method
Put washed rose petals in a saucepan with water and bring
to a boil. Simmer for ten minutes, then add the sugar, stirring all the time. After the sugar has completely dissolved,
add the lemon juice and zest. Simmer for another ten
minutes. Do the cold saucer test to see if the jam sets. If it
doesn't, add the ½ bottle of liquid pectin and simmer for
ten minutes, stirring all the time. After, pour the jam into
warm, sterilised jars. Put lids on immediately.

Peach and Lavender Jam
Ingredients
6 peaches, chopped
2 tablespoons of lavender buds (crushed)
500 grams / 1 pound of jam sugar with added pectin
½ lemon, zested and juiced
½ bottle of liquid pectin

Method

Put all ingredients (except the liquid pectin) in a deep saucepan and bring slowly to a boil. Keep stirring all the time before reducing the heat. Cook for about twenty minutes, occasionally stirring. Do a saucer test for setting. If it sets, ladle into warm, sterilised jars. If not, add the liquid pectin and boil down another ten minutes, stirring all the time. When the jam is at setting consistency, ladle into warm, sterilised jars. Put lids on right away.

Pineapple Jam

Pineapples and mangos feel like summer. Their refreshing tastes quench the thirst of hot, lazy summer days. This jam is for pineapple, but mangos are interchangeable. Both jams are delicious on toast or ice cream.

Ingredients

1 medium-size fresh pineapple, peeled and diced
500 grams / 1 pound of jam sugar with added pectin
2 fresh lemons, zested and juiced

Method

Put all ingredients into a deep saucepan and boil for about ten minutes, then reduce the heat and simmer for about an hour. With a hand blender or potato masher, crush the fruit to bite-size pieces. Ladle into sterilised jars and put lids on immediately.

If substituting mangos, use four to five good-size mangos cut into chunks.

Lavender Marmalade

Just as with lemon, oranges make a good combination with lavender.

Ingredients

4 tablespoons of dried lavender flowers
50 millilitres / 0.2 cup of warm water
6 oranges
1 kilogram / 4 cups of preserving sugar or jam sugar

Soak the lavender flowers in warm water for ten minutes, then strain (this is the norm when cooking with lavender). Wash the oranges and cut them into quarters. Put them in a blender and chop until finely ground, skin and all. Then boil the oranges with the sugar and lavender for about twenty minutes, stirring occasionally. Fill sterilised jars with the mixture and screw the tops on. Leave the marmalade to completely cool before putting it in the fridge, where it will keep for six months.

Another good combination is apples and lavender. The possibilities with lavender are endless. Experiment and substitute it with other herbs in various dishes.

THE JELLIES

The summer garden is when flowers come into their own. There are just as many flowers to make jellies with as there are herbs, yet we often overlook flowers when we think of jellies.

Flower jellies are perfect as an addition to sweets, while herbs are perfect with savoury dishes. Tastes differ, so try everything. Jellies are great with cheeses and cold meats, such as ham, turkey, duck, and pheasant. A lovely, big dollop of peony jelly with a slice of cold turkey or duck and freshly baked, crusty bread is rather delicious this time of year.

Experiment with flowers and flavours for your jellies, but follow the standard recipe for Lilac Jelly. Moreover, savoury jellies require gelatine to solidify, but for flower jellies, I have chosen to stay with pectin, as flower jellies are supposed to be light and sweet. Also, use smaller jars for jellies, as you would not use as much jelly as jam or marmalade.

Lilac Jelly

Ingredients

450 grams/4 cups of lilac flowers, washed

1 litre/4 cups of water

450 grams/4 cups of sugar

3 tablespoons of lemon juice

6 tablespoons of powdered pectin

Method

Put flowers and water in a pan and boil for about a half hour before turning off the heat. Cover and leave overnight, allowing the flowers to steep. The next day, strain the water and discard the flowers. Return water to the pan and add sugar and lemon juice. Bring to a boil, making sure the sugar has dissolved, then simmer for thirty minutes before adding the pectin, either powdered or liquid. Simmer for ten minutes. Check with the cold saucer test. If it's not setting, cook for another ten minutes before checking again. When ready, ladle into sterilised jam jars.

Peony Jelly

Ingredients

450 grams / 4 cups of peony flowers, petals washed
1 litre / 4 cups of water
345 grams / 3 cups of sugar
2 tablespoons of powdered gelatine or liquid pectin
3 tablespoons of lemon juice, freshly squeezed

Method

Boil the peony petals in the water for about thirty minutes. Leave overnight. In the morning, strain and discard the petals and add the lemon juice to the water. Bring to a boil and add the sugar and pectin. Boil for ten minutes before ladling into sterilised jars.

Violet Jelly

Ingredients
450 grams/4 cups of violet flowers
1 litre/4 cups of water
1 tablespoon of lemon juice
450 grams/4 cups of sugar
1 packet/30 grams of powdered pectin or half a bottle of
   liquid pectin

Method
Use the method for Lilac Jelly. Always let flowers steep overnight or for a full twenty-four hours. The key to good flower jelly is the steeping of flowers. Further, adding the lemon juice will change the colour to a pink, but if you want to keep the blue, don't use any. If you don't have many violet flowers, then half the ingredients will make a small batch. Remember, for jellies, always use a small jar, then you can make more gifts, and so on.

Lemon and Lavender Jelly

Ingredients

2 tablespoons of lavender flowers, dried or fresh

3 tablespoons of lemon zest

700 millilitres / 3 cups of lemon juice

30 grams / 2 ounces of powdered gelatine or liquid pectin

350 grams / 2.5 cups of jam sugar with added pectin

Method

Boil all the ingredients together (except the pectin and sugar) for about fifteen minutes, then put the pot's lid on and let steep for fifteen to twenty minutes. After, you can strain the lavender out, but I keep it in, as it adds to the texture of the jelly. After straining (if you choose to do so), boil the mixture again and add the pectin and sugar. Boil for another ten minutes before pouring into warm, sterilised jars.

If the jellies do not set after two hours, boil again and add thirty grams of gelatine to the mixture. Don't forget to sterilise the jars again.

THE CHUTNEYS

Chutney is a wonderful resource to have in the cupboard as it is so versatile. It can be used on its own as a side dish to add flavour with cheese and cold meats. It can be used in stews, casseroles, pasta sauces, and curries to add texture, flavour, and that little something extra. The making of chutneys appears in the seasonal to-do list as we want to harness the fruits and vegetables of summer.

The chutneys listed here are all unique to summer but can be stored in a cool, dark place until Yule or Christmas. Always use material to cover the lid, as it gives an old, worldly charm to homemade products.

Chutneys always taste better if they have been left for at least a couple of weeks before being used. They seem to get better with age. All these chutneys will last at least six months if stored in the fridge after opening. The vinegar acts as a preservative. Nevertheless, always date whatever you make, and never leave anything longer than a year if possible.

The key to making chutney is to keep stirring it. This helps the moisture evaporate through steam, and this is what we want. Try to do this on a clear, cool day with all windows open, as making chutney can be a bit smelly, and the house can smell of vinegar even days after!

Peach Chutney
Ingredients
2 onions

5 peaches, stoned and chopped

1 large red pepper, chopped

1 teaspoon of ground ginger

1 teaspoon of ground cinnamon

1 teaspoon of ground cloves

1 teaspoon of nutmeg

250 grams/2 cups of sultanas

700 millilitres/3 cups of apple cider vinegar

350 grams/2.5 cups of brown sugar

Method
In a deep saucepan, fry the onions with a little olive oil until soft and translucent. Add the ginger and pepper and stir. Add the rest of the ingredients and boil for at least twenty minutes.

As it's still boiling, begin stirring, allowing the moisture to evaporate through steam. Keep stirring for at least ten to twenty minutes. The mixture will start to become very thick.

A good way to test chutney is to drag the spoon through the middle. If it doesn't immediately fill with liquid, it is done. If it does fill with liquid, it needs more cooking.

When the chutney is cooked, ladle into warm, sterilised jars and cover immediately. Label and date the jars.

If the chutney is still a bit runny, simply boil again, and make sure to evaporate the moisture.

Eggplant Chutney

Ingredients

2 cups of baby eggplants, chopped

1 cup of sultanas

2 medium onions, chopped

3 tablespoons of tomato paste

2 garlic cloves, crushed

2 red chillies, deseeded and thinly sliced
1 tablespoon of coriander seeds, crushed coarsely
1 teaspoon of mustard
700 millilitres/3 cups of apple cider vinegar
350 grams/2.5 cups of demerara sugar

Method
Follow the method for Peach Chutney, but simmer ingredients for at least forty minutes to ensure the eggplant is properly cooked before beginning the stirring process.

Don't forget to warm jars in the oven while the chutney is cooking.

Onion and Pineapple Chutney
Ingredients
1 large fresh pineapple, chopped into chunks
1 cup of sultanas
5 medium onions, chopped
1 teaspoon of white pepper
1 teaspoon of mustard
3 tablespoons of chopped root ginger
2 garlic cloves, crushed

2 red chillies, deseeded and thinly sliced

1 teaspoon of paprika

700 millilitres/3 cups of apple cider vinegar or white
vinegar

350 grams/2.5 cups of demerara sugar or brown sugar

Method

Follow the method of Peach Chutney, but simmer ingredients for at least twenty minutes to ensure all ingredients
are properly cooked before beginning the stirring process.

Remember, the perfect chutney is syrupy and thick,
with no runny liquid.

Plum and Ginger Chutney

Ingredients

1 kilogram/5 cups of plums, quartered and stones
removed

350 grams/2.5 cups of sultanas

2 medium onions, chopped

1 pear, peeled, cored, and chopped

1 apple, peeled, cored, and chopped

3 tablespoons of chopped root ginger

4 garlic cloves, crushed
2 red chillies, deseeded and thinly sliced
500 millilitres/2 cups of apple cider vinegar
350 grams/2.5 cups of demerara sugar

Method
Just as with the previous chutney methods, fry up the onion, then add the ginger, chillies, and cloves. Fry for three to five minutes, releasing the aromatic scents before adding the plums. Stir in the sugar and vinegar. Boil for at least thirty minutes, stirring occasionally, ensuring the chutney is not burning at the bottom of the pan. After, ladle into warm, sterilised jars, and always remember to label with a date.

Nectarine and Tomato Chutney
Ingredients
6 nectarines, chopped
4 plum tomatoes, chopped
250 millilitres/1 cup of apple cider vinegar
150 grams/1 cup of brown sugar
½ cup of dried peaches, diced

½ cup of raisins

1 onion, chopped

2 teaspoons of mustard seeds

2 garlic cloves, crushed

1 chopped chile

4 peppercorns

Method

Place all the ingredients in a large bowl and refrigerate overnight. The next day, pour the entire mixture into a large saucepan and bring it to a boil. Keep stirring all the time. Reduce to a medium heat and cook for at least forty to forty-five minutes, stirring quite often. Don't let the mixture burn. When it is shiny and glossy and there is no excessive moisture left, it is ready. Ladle into sterilised jam or chutney jars.

THE SYRUPS

The summer is a beautiful time of heady scents and aromatic herbs releasing their fragrances all day and evening. These gifts of nature are crammed with vitamins and minerals—all the essential immune-boosting ingredients human bodies need to fight the coming autumn and winter. Here, we are going to make some of my favourites: Honeysuckle Syrup, Lavender Syrup, and Rose Petal Syrup, among others—not to mention the famous Violet Decoction.

Violets were used in the Middle Ages to cure all ailments of the lungs; many flowers were grown not only for aesthetic considerations, but for their medicinal and culinary uses. M. Maeterllinck details their medicinal uses:

> *Violet; The Decoction of violets is good against hoate feuers, and the inflammation of the liver and all other inward partes, driuing forth … the hoate and cholerique humors. The like properie hath the iuice, syrupe, or conserue of the same. The syrupe of violets is good against the inflammation of the lunges and breast, and against pleurise, and cough, and also against feuers or Agues, but especially in young children.*
>
> *The same syrupe cureth all inflammation and roughness of the throte if it be much let or often holden*

in the mouth. The sugar if violets, and also the conserue and iuyce, bringeth the same to passe.[6]

I am going to teach you how to make a decoction of violets for you to use when you have "inflammation of the lunges." However, always see a doctor first. The ingredients may counteract your regular medication. Further, you may have unknown allergies to the compounds found in certain plants, so always err on the side of caution.

Violet Decoction

Ingredients

250 grams / 2 cups of sugar

250 millilitres / 2 cups of water

1 teaspoon of lemon juice (optional)

500 grams / 4 cups of violet flowers, washed with stems and green leaves removed (we just want the flower petals)

....
6. Frank Crisp, *Medieval Garden* (New York: Hacker Art Books, 1979), 47.

Method

Put the violets and water in a pan and simmer for about ten minutes. Remove from the heat, cover with the lid, and allow to steep for at least twenty-four hours. After, strain the flowers from the liquid by using a sieve and gently press any liquid from the flowers, then discard them. Pop the water back in the pan and add the sugar gradually. Bring to a gentle simmer (if you boil this water, you will lose the blue colour), stirring all the time as to not burn the sugar. If you want to keep the blue colour, do not add the lemon juice. When cool, pour into sterilised glass bottles and store in the refrigerator for up to six months—just in time to give as Christmas presents if you make it in June or July (if the violets last that long).

Honeysuckle Syrup
Ingredients

50 honeysuckle flowers, washed

250 millilitres / 1 cup of water

100 grams / 1 cup of sugar

Method

In a pan, add all the ingredients and boil for about ten minutes before reducing the heat and allowing to simmer for five minutes. Turn off the heat and cover. Allow the mixture to steep and cool completely before straining and discarding the flowers. Pour liquid into sterilised glass bottles. Don't forget to label and date the syrup. Use within one month.

Rosemary Syrup

Ingredients

100 grams/1 cup of fresh rosemary, washed
250 millilitres/1 cup of water
100 grams/1 cup of sugar

Method

Put all ingredients into a pan and boil for about twenty minutes, then remove from the heat, cover, and allow to steep for at least an hour before straining and removing the rosemary. Pour the syrup into sterilised glass bottles and store in the fridge for up to a month. Don't forget to label and date.

You can use different types of herbs and herb combinations to make a syrup; just be aware that some herbs, such as sage, are overpowering, so limit the quantity.

Lavender Syrup
Ingredients
250 grams/2 cups of sugar
500 millilitres/2 cups of water
2 tablespoons of lavender
1 tablespoon of blueberries

Method
Put all ingredients in a pan and boil, stirring all the time to dissolve the sugar. Lower heat to a simmer and cook for ten minutes. Remove from the heat and cover with a lid. Allow syrup to completely cool before straining the liquid to remove the lavender and blueberries. After, pour into sterilised glass bottles and store in the refrigerator for up to a month.

Rose Petal Syrup

Ingredients

100 millilitres / 1 cup of water

200 grams / 1 cup of sugar

200 grams / 1 cup of rose petals, washed

1 teaspoon of lemon juice

Method

Put the water and rose petals in a saucepan and simmer for about twenty minutes before removing from the heat and allowing to cool. Steep for at least an hour. Strain the rose petals and return the liquid to the pan, adding the sugar. Gently bring to a simmer, stirring all the time. Add lemon juice and see what happens to the colour when you do. Pour into sterilised glass bottles and refrigerate for up to six months.

Sloe Gin

Sloes are the fruit of the blackthorn, a flowering plant of the rose family. They are native to Europe, Western Asia, New

Zealand, and eastern North America. If sloes do not grow where you live, substitute either blueberries or cherries.

Ingredients
500 grams / 4 cups of ripe sloes, washed and dried
250 grams / 2 cups of granulated or caster sugar
1 litre / 4 cups of gin

Method
Wash the sloes well and tip them into a two-litre glass jar or divide them between two smaller jars. Add the sugar and gin, then seal the jar. Shake well. Once a day for seven days, give the jar a good shake. Store the jar in a cool, dark place and leave for two to three months; the longer, the better.

After, line a plastic sieve with a square of muslin set over a bowl and strain the sloe gin through it. Decant into clean, dry bottles, then seal and label. Use as and when needed.

Lavender Lemonade

Ingredients

500 millilitres/2 cups of water

200 grams/1 cup of sugar

1 tablespoon of dried or fresh lavender (if fresh, make sure to wash)

250 millilitres/1 cup of lemon juice

500 millilitres/2 cups of cold water or sparkling mineral water

Ice cubes

Method

In a large saucepan, boil sugar, lavender, and water for about fifteen minutes, stirring all the time to make sure the sugar dissolves. Cover and let stand for at least an hour. After, strain, discarding the lavender flowers (or keep them in, if you prefer). Add the cold and/or sparkling mineral water. Mix well and serve over ice.

From the Cauldron

The summer crafts and spells are dominated by the nature around us, and flowers and leaves make a wonderful addition to the décor of any home. Pressing flowers and leaves becomes the evening pastime for me, along with performing spells outside.

SUMMER CRAFTS

One of the best pastimes of summer is flower pressing and leaf pressing. This hobby ensures that the flowers you have in summer can be treasured all year. They are a valuable resource and can be made into so many gifts.

Preserving Leaves

Here is one way to preserve beautiful, lush, green leaves, which we are going to need for a number of craft projects. Preserve them by placing them flat in a clear bag and coating them in a water and vegetable glycerine mixture: ½ cup of water, ¼ cup of vegetable glycerine. Make sure all leaves are covered and keep them in the bag for three to four days with the solution, then take them out and leave them to dry for twenty-four hours. Another way is to dip the leaves in melted paraffin wax and leave them to dry. This makes the leaves rather stiff and hard, whereas the glycerine is much softer and pliable for craft projects.

Leaf Glass Mandalas

You Will Need

A flower press or heavy books

A selection of leaves, fresh or glycerine

Double-sided tape

Picture frames

Use the glycerine leaves or an old-fashioned flower press and press the leaves you have found. After, arrange them on a glass hanging frame and secure with double-sided tape. Always play with the arrangement of your leaves on the glass frame before you secure with the tape—it will look a mess if you keep rearranging with the tape.

After, hang your leaf glass mandalas around the home—they look extra cool hanging at a window, as they look like stained glass nature windows, and they are so beautiful when the light shines through them. You could also create flower petal mandalas for a pretty flower window this season.

Midsummer Rose Potpourri

You Will Need

Rose petals

A selection of essential oils

Bowl

Newspaper

A selection of spices (nutmeg, cinnamon, cloves, allspice)

The best way to dry rose petals is in the sun, not the oven, as they lose most of their colour that way, and in potpourri, the colour is just as important as the smell. Pick your roses in the morning of a dry, sunny day and spread the petals out on a piece of newspaper. Leave until the evening. The rose petals need to be completely dry, otherwise rot will set in later.

Pop the petals in a paper bag along with nutmeg, cinnamon, cloves, and allspice and give a good shake. You can add ribbons, glitter, and all the other lovely bits and bobs in your potpourri at this stage; just pop it all in the bag and shake up. Then add a couple of drops of rose essential oil. Give a good shake before popping the potpourri in a glass jar with a lid for about a week to seal in the aroma. Then use as and when needed to scent your home.

You can use as many different types of flower leaves to add to your rose petals, but always make sure they are completely dried. There are many ways to dry flowers, like the old oven way: Cut the stems, leaving only the flowers, and space evenly on an oven rack. Set the oven between 150 and 200 degrees and bake the flowers for 1.5 to 2.5 hours. Let them cool, and then they are ready to use for all crafts and potpourri.

Summer Mermaid Crystal Shells
You Will Need
Shells
Gloves
4 tablespoons of borax
1 cup of water
Clean jam jars

Collect shells on the beach. Only collect what you need, as sea creatures also need these shells for homes. The same is true with all projects: only take what you need. If the item is on the ground, do not pull, break, or dig up anything in order to have it for your nature collection. If you don't find what you are looking for, maybe you are not meant to make that project, or perhaps you are meant to come up with another idea!

This is a fun activity and a great science project. Boil the water and add the borax. Mix well. Pop the seashells into clean jam jars and pour the borax mixture over them, making sure to cover them completely. Leave for twenty-four hours, and then carefully take out the shells and leave them to dry. Use your crystal seashells for a range of decorative and craft projects, from creating a display in the bathroom, to adding sparkle to a mermaid-themed potpourri centrepiece.

Lavender Bath Soak

You Will Need

200 grams / 1 cup of Dead Sea salt

200 grams / 1 cup of Himalayan pink salt

100 grams / ½ cup of baking soda

100 grams / ½ cup of lavender flowers

100 grams / ½ cup of French green clay

10 drops of lavender essential oil

Method

Layer all salts, baking soda, and clay in a mason jar, making sure to put the flowers on top before adding the essential oil. Pop the lid on. This looks beautiful as a gift or standing on a bathroom shelf.

Another way is to mix everything up in a bowl and scoop the mixture into circular pieces of muslin or muslin bags. Tie the bags up with ribbon and add them to the bath while the tap is running. Gorgeous little gifts for friends, especially if you make a mermaid gift basket.

SUMMER SPELLS

Summer spells are predominately performed outside, weather permitting, and focus on nature and elementals. If you can, try to create a special place in your garden where you can perform spells and summer rituals without disturbance.

Midsummer Magic Fae Invite

On Midsummer, leave some tiny pieces of cake, honey and water in a thimble or little jug, a couple of flowers, anything bell-shaped, and perhaps some moss in your special place. If you are lucky enough to already have a fairy ring (a round, bare patch or round area of daisies, dandelions, mushrooms, or toadstools) growing, then lucky you. Place the gifts in the fairy ring or special place and say this spell:

> *On this day and on this night,*
> *to the world of fae I invite.*
> *Come now upon this hour.*
> *Fly from your fairy bower.*
> *Feel free here to roam,*

in my garden, but not in my home.
These gifts I leave for you, I implore.
But feel free to leave me anything more.

Stay awhile in your garden and leave the cake and honey water for the fae. Leave the gifts for a full twenty-four hours. If they are gone the next day, then well done! You have the fae now entering your garden, but do not invite them inside. They belong to nature and are not house-trained at all! You have been warned!

You may start finding little gifts in your garden, from buttons, to old coins, to shiny objects. These are gifts from the fae. Believe it or not, you may even find gold rings in the strangest of places, such as growing on a tree or in the centre of a rosebush!

Bee's Knees of Magic

There is a little life force that works for all on this planet: flora, fauna, and humans alike. This little bee-ing is simply that … a bee. These important insects pollinate the world, and yet they are becoming endangered. Please do not let that happen. By planting just a couple of these herbs in your garden, window boxes, and patios, we can begin to save the habitats of these wonderous miracle workers.

Here are some plants that help bee colonies:

Herbs
bee balm, borage, catnip, cilantro, fennel, lavender, mints, rosemary, sage, thyme

Plants
buttercups, clematis, dahlias, English ivy, foxglove, globe thistle, hollyhocks, marigolds, rock cress, roses, snowdrops, sunflowers, yellow hyssop

Save the Planet Spell
Even if you just fill a window box or patio pot with cat mint or lavender, know that you are helping to save the planet. Every little bit of gardening we do goes a long way in creating food for the world's greatest pollinator. As you water your plants, say,

> *Black and yellow,*
> *yellow and black.*

We will give nature back.
I plant this flower for Mr. Bee,
helping this world, you and me.

Lammas Spell

In your sacred place in the garden, create your little altar and adorn it with a corn dolly, if you can, or some pieces of corn, wheat, or barley and a fresh jar of honey. A fresh loaf is the centrepiece, and perhaps a sunflower also can adorn your altar, along with a fireproof bowl of water and a small bowl of salt, a cup of mead, or white wine. Light one orange candle and one yellow candle and raise your arms toward the sky. Say,

Lammas, fair and wise,
thank you for the summer skies.
Bounty of the harvest first,
wheat and barley, quenches thirst.
Blessed be to these fruits of bread and honey.
Blessed be to the weather, fair and sunny.
Changing seasons, changing fast.
These blessings of yours will last.

Raise your wine to the sky and garden in toast, and then drink. Meditate at your altar and think about all the good times and all the good things that have happened to you during the summer. If you made a summer to-do list, now is the time to tick items off. Look at the list as you meditate on things you completed, and then burn the list with the orange candle before dropping it into the bowl of water. Sprinkle the water and list remains on the garden.

Well Dressing Healing Water Spell

Wells are the symbolic embodiment of Mother Earth from which the healing waters arise. We need water to survive, and we are made of water. In honour of well dressing this month, create a healing elixir using crystals.

The best stone to use for healing is amethyst. This crystal is often called the all-healer and is beneficial for people, animals, and plants. It is especially beneficial for those who suffer from migraines and headaches and is often called nature's tranquillizer.

Make an amethyst elixir by first cleaning the stone. Do not use bleach or other chemicals when cleaning crystals. Simply place the amethyst in hot water for a couple of minutes. Then place the clean amethyst into drinking water and let it soak for a few hours. As the stone is soaking, say these words:

> *Healing energy, flow to me.*
> *Earth and water.*
> *So, mote it be.*

Take out the stone, then use the water in drinks or on pulse points. Give what is left to plants and make fresh amethyst water every day.

Staycation Spell

Not everyone can go away on holiday, and many of us have a staycation. We stay in our local neighbourhoods. This can also prove to be an adventure. Go out into your local area and check your local tourist office or visit your local library. There may have been a great battle where you live. There may be something of great historical and national importance. Research your home or begin to research your family tree. A staycation in not a bad thing, as you can find information you would never have otherwise known. Use the time to see the magic and wonder in your local neighbourhood.

If you are not going anywhere, say this spell the night before your vacation is due to start. Light a blue candle and say these words:

Here in my block,
show me the wonders I do not see.
Show me the sights of fantasy.
Here in my neighbourhood are castles and magic.
There is mystery and wonder in my vicinity.
I shall see all here in my block.
An' it harm none, so mote it be.

SUMMER ELEMENTALS

The summer elementals that we can encounter during June, July, and August are as varied as they are marvellous. During the summer, water elementals predominate, such as mermaids, nereids, and selkies. The sea holds such mystery and power that it captivates us, and these watery elementals are immortal beings who can spend an eternity at sea. There is also one elemental that predominates this time of year: the nymph of nature and forests.

Mermaids

The one thing about merfolk that cannot be denied is that they certainly know how to look after themselves. This can lead to some people calling them vain, yet we must all look after ourselves, for if we do not, then we cannot take care of others.

Merpeople have been around for thousands of years and are recorded all over the world, from Japan, to Scandinavia, to Babylonia, to Mesopotamia. There are figures of humans with a fish's tail in ancient writings, and in the stories of the Arabian Nights, there is the story of Abdullah the fisherman and Abdullah the merman. In Syria, there are many stories of merpeople and especially of a merman who had a human wife; the subsequent child, a son, spoke the language of both the land and the sea. Now that's bilingual!

The British Isles are littered with stories of mermaids and mortals falling in love, from Cornwall to Scotland; indeed, one Scottish clan claims to be descended from a mermaid. The stories stemming from the British Isles regarding the merfolk are endless, but then again, we are completely surrounded by water. Denmark is also a series of islands, and let us not forget the most famous mermaid whose statue now graces the Copenhagen harbour. The North Sea and Atlantic Ocean around Scandinavia have their fair share of similar legends. These mysterious elementals of water are indeed magical.

The stones and crystals we use to connect with the merpeople are larimar (the stone of Atlantis), water sapphire, paua shell, and, of course, pearls. Another lesser-known stone for the connection to merpeople is neptunite, which is named after the Roman god of the sea, Neptune (though this stone is rather rare and very expensive).

Mermaid Connection

If you would like to connect with the elemental mermaid, buy a piece of larimar or pearls. (Please do not buy coral as the world's coral is an endangered species. If you have inherited one, it can be used.) Holding the gemstone in your hands, say,

> *Stone of the sea, I call to thee.*
> *Mermaids I wish to see.*
> *In dreams or reality.*

Keep the stone on your person if it is a ring or piece of jewellery. If it's just a single pearl or piece of larimar, keep it with you in your purse. If you are lucky enough to go to the coast or seaside for a vacation, keep a lookout for the merfolk. At night, sleep with the stone underneath your pillow to enhance your dreams of mermaids.

Nymphs

The other elemental being of summer is the nymph. The lovely nymphs are a personification of nature, as they are spirit manifested in nature itself. Nymphs are tree spirits who protect the forests, the woods, and the eternal springs of life. They cherish and nurture nature and celebrate death as a renewal of life. Nymphs stem from Greek mythology and are regarded as semidivine. You could call them the daughters of Gaia, for the earth is theirs to protect and care for. They are indeed the natural florists of the world, and many hedgewitches work with nymph energies.

As nymphs are the personification of nature, they are also very much aware of the pleasures of the flesh. Sexuality is a part of nature, not just in the act of procreation, but in the expression of love toward another. Nymphs, of course, love to frolic and be free; they are freedom-loving, wild, and sensual beings who are in tune with their own sexuality.

Nymph Connection

To enjoy and tune in to this wonderful energy is to express your sensuality and be confident with your own sexuality. Placing certain crystals and stones around the bedroom can enhance the pleasure and connection that comes with sex. One of the main stones for this is Shiva lingam. This stone unites and strengthens the sexual union between people. If you have been having problems with your partner, this is the stone to place in your bedroom. It is also particularly good for fertility issues, so place one in your bedroom if you are trying to conceive. This stone is beneficial for those who wish to practise sacred or tantric spiritual sex.

If the libido has been dwindling as of late, another stone to use is red tiger's eye or a ruby. Place these in the bedroom and see what happens. Moss agate works well with the energy of the nymphs and is another stone for creating a harmonious and long-lasting relationship. You can also use tree agate; its proper name is dendritic agate, as it was named after the word for tree in Greek. Tree agate is particularly good to use when we want to connect directly with the nymphs.

Another way you can tune in to the nymphs is to learn the meanings of flowers. Some call it the language of flowers, and it is used to predict future events. A bit like tea reading, but it is flower reading instead. Here are some flower meanings:

Camelia: This beautiful flower means the birth of a new baby or receiving news of a baby.

Daisy: The daisy is one of the first flowers of spring. It is said that if you see three daisies growing together, then spring has sprung. As a result, the meaning for this flower is that of new beginnings, including motherhood, children, a new job, or a new house.

Honeysuckle: This heavenly scented flower means that a wish will be granted. Whatever you desire will shortly find its way to you.

Rose: This eternal flower means love, whether it be for a person, place, or job. It is a flower that signifies deep desire, longing, and respect. However, this beautiful flower can also mean sorrow and grief, so be on your guard if you feel drawn to a rose.

Nereids

Nereids are not to be confused with the rather vain mermaid, nor with the highly sexualised nymphs of the forests. Although they are cousins of these, nereids are the gentler, more compassionate elemental of the sea. They feature in Greek mythology, and it is said they are the daughters of Nereus and Doris. There are fifty nereids, and they represent the beauty of the sea. They sing beautifully, but they are not to be confused with the sirens, who lure lost sailors to their deaths with their singing. Instead, the nereid is said to save drowning sailors and safely bring them to land.

Nereid Connection

If you are feeling sad and upset, call upon the compassionate nature of the nereids for comfort and support by creating a healing bath salt mixture. In a mason jar, place one cup of Epsom salts and three star anises with four drops of cypress oil. Secure with a lid. Shake the jar up, then place it in a bowl of water overnight. Place both hands on the bowl and say,

> *Nereids, I call to thee.*
> *Sisters eternal of the sea.*
> *Bring love and harmony.*
> *Forever in this bath mix for me.*

In the morning, take the jar out of the bowl and throw the water on the garden. Keep the jar in your bathroom and sprinkle a couple of tablespoons in your bathwater when you are feeling upset. Relax, and let the salt water soothe you.

SUMMER ESBAT RITUAL

During the summer months, our full moon Esbat ritual focuses on the earth. If you want to focus your thoughts on actively helping the earth by recycling or planting bee-friendly plants, say this prayer before you commence any work in the garden. Incite the energies of the earth by saying this prayer on the first night of the full moon.

In your garden—bare feet and open palms firmly placed on the earth—call to the earth with a prayer for dedication and healing. Imagine people all over the world saying and doing the same thing, and see in your mind how the earth can be transformed into Eden once more:

Earth, hear my call.
Planet of my birth, I owe you all.
I pray for the sun and the rain.
Thank you for the wild and the tame.

Thank you for the flowers, plants, and trees.
The gifts of seasons you've given to me.
I pray for rebirth, renewal, and energy.
I will be there for you when you need me the most.
Healing of the earth begins now, from coast to coast.

Give thanks for everything the earth has given you so far, and make an offering of the first fruit of your summer harvest or leave some strawberries on your summer altar.

SUMMER SEASONAL CORRESPONDENCE CHART

In addition to the correspondences mentioned in this chapter, there are others we can use:

Colours: Reds, yellows, greens, blues

Crystals: Goldstone, sunstone

Flowers: Roses, sunflowers, delphiniums, dianthus, gladiolas

Incense: Rose, lotus, grapefruit

Oils: Lavender, lemon, rosemary
Weather: Sun, tropical heatwave, rain
Deities: Aphrodite, Apollo, Poseidon
Elementals: Mermaids, nymphs, unicorns
Planets: Mercury, Earth, Sun
Numbers: 2, 4, 8

Autumn

The three months of autumn—September, October, and November—bring their unique weather and magical emphasis to us. The September festival of Mabon, the autumnal equinox, brings a unique power to the world. It is not like the vernal equinox of the spring, which promises new life and renewed energies; the autumnal equinox brings a deeper and, some might say, darker power to spells and all magical practices that we adhere to during the month of September. It can be argued that Mabon is a precursor to the renowned festival of Samhain, otherwise known as Halloween, which we find in October, a month of tumultuous weather.

The October hurricanes around the world bring much devastation, and our healing thoughts must go to our kin across the seas during these times. You will find here a section on the weather in which a healing prayer is said for those who experience such devastating natural force.

In the northern hemisphere, November brings the mists and fog, which shut down many city airports. And yet this mysterious weather phenomenon, which can bring death and destruction, ironically is also a powerful vehicle hedgewitches can use to travel to the other realms. Therefore, a travelling spell can also be found in the spell section of this chapter.

NATURE'S BOUNTY: AUTUMN

Here is just a selection of the fruits and vegetables available in autumn:

apples, angelica, basil, bay leaf, beans, beetroot, blackberries, blueberries, borage, broccoli, Brussel sprouts, cabbage, carrots, cauliflower, celeriac, celery, chard, chamomile, chicory, chives, courgettes, crab apples, cranberries, cress, cucumber, dill, eggplants, endive, fennel, figs, garlic, garlic chives, grapes, Jerusalem artichoke, kale, kohl rabi, lamb's lettuce, lavender, leeks, lemon balm, lettuce, loganberry, lovage, marjoram, marrows, medlar, melon, mint, mushrooms, onions, oregano, parsley, parsnips, peas, pears, peppers, plums, potatoes, pumpkins, quince, red cabbage, rocket lettuce, raspberries, rosemary, rosehips, runner beans, sage, shallots, sorrel, spinach, squash, swede, turnips, thyme, tomatoes, winter white radishes

From the Kitchen

The hedgewitch's day is a busy one in autumn, and for that matter, so are the nights! I am busy gathering and collecting as much of nature's bounty as I can. The fruits of autumn make wonderful jams and jellies, while the vegetables and herbs make delicious chutneys that can be used throughout the coming winter months.

THE JAMS

The fruits of autumn are a blessing and are not to be wasted whatsoever. Use as much of them as you can. Make sure to save jam jars and other mason jars all summer as autumn soon comes around with its bountiful harvest.

The fruits most prevalent in autumn are:

plums, damsons, apples, brambles, medlar, quince, black currants, and pears, to name but a few. Depending on where you live, these are readily available in the supermarket. But nothing compares to fresh fruit, so please try to use every plum, pear, or apple from the tree. It is even better if you can pick the fruit yourself, as the longer you have the fruit, the more power you are placing upon it.

Here are some key autumn jam recipes from a hedge-witch. Always be careful when cooking jams, as they can suddenly burn if you leave them too long, so make sure to watch the pan and keep stirring. If you do happen to burn a batch of jam, call it Autumn Jam, reminiscent of toffee apples and bonfire nights; plum jam is particularly good for burning and creating the taste of toffee apples if it gets burnt.

Rhubarb and Plum Jam

Ingredients

700 grams / 1.5 pounds of trimmed rhubarb, thinly sliced

500 grams / 1 pound of plums, quartered and stones removed

600 grams / 1.3 pounds of jam sugar with added pectin

½ bottle of liquid pectin

1 teaspoon of butter

A splash of cranberry juice

Method

Put fruit and sugar in a deep saucepan. Some people buy a special preserving pan, but don't go to the expense. Add a splash of water or cranberry juice (just enough so that the fruit and sugar don't burn). The fruit itself will release its own juices quickly once it starts cooking, so don't put too much extra liquid in. Keep stirring until the sugar has dissolved and bring to a boil. Keep boiling for about ten to fifteen minutes. Stir occasionally to prevent burning.

Add a teaspoon of butter to the boiling mixture and stir through.

If you like the taste of fruit and there are still some larger pieces of undissolved plum, keep the jam as it is. If you prefer a smoother jam, blast it with a hand blender or potato masher while cooking.

After the jam has reached its setting point, ladle it into warm, sterilised jars, right to the top. Screw on lids over waxed discs or cellophane tops secured with elastic bands. Decorate with a traditional material covering the top. Leave to cool, then label and date. Store in a cool place.

Autumn Nights Jam
Ingredients
3 apples, washed and diced
3 pears, washed and diced
400 grams / 1.5 cups of blackberries (always soak freshly
    picked blackberries beforehand)

400 grams / 1.5 cups of plums, quartered and stones
   removed
600 grams / 2.5 cups of jam sugar with added pectin
2 teaspoons of freshly chopped ginger (optional)
½ bottle of liquid pectin
1 teaspoon of butter
A splash of cranberry or orange juice

Method
Put all fruit, sugar, and ginger in a pan and bring to a boil.
Follow the Rhubarb and Plum Jam method.

Hedgerow Jam

This is a generic recipe for all manner of fruits and berries
found in the hedgerow, which is a mixed hedge of wild
shrubs, plants, and trees bordering a road or field. Hedge-
rows are usually found in the countryside. On an autumn
day, go outside and collect what you can find. The blackberries and raspberries can be substituted for rowan,
elderberries, and plums or damsons—whatever you find.

Ingredients

8 ounces / 1 cup of rosehips

1 pound / 4 cups of sloes or blueberries or plums

2 pounds / 8 cups of crab apples

8 ounces / 1 cup of blackberries and raspberries

Sugar with added pectin

A splash of water or cranberry juice

Method

Wash and clean the fruit. Put the rosehips, sloes, or substitutes and the chopped crab apples into a preserving pan. Add water or cranberry juice to cover and cook slowly until all the fruits are tender: usually about forty minutes to one hour. Pass the fruit mixture through a jam strainer or sieve. Keep the liquid, weigh it, and pour it into a large saucepan. Add the same amount of sugar as there is liquid. Also add the blackberries and raspberries to the pan and simmer for fifteen minutes, or until the mixture reaches its setting point. Pour into warm, sterilised jars and put lids on immediately.

Fall Hedgewitch Jam

Ingredients

500 grams/2 cups of apples

500 grams/2 cups of pears

250 grams/1 cup of rowan berries

500 grams/2 cups of sugar with added pectin

1 teaspoon of ground cinnamon

3 cloves

2 limes

Method

Peel and quarter the apples and pears, removing the seeds and core, then finely dice. Rinse and drain the rowan berries. Mix together with the juice of one lime, sugar, spices, apples, and pears. Leave overnight to infuse.

Rinse the second lime in hot water and remove the peel. Squeeze all the juice out and add it to the fruit mixture. Put in a pan and bring to a boil, stirring constantly. Cook for ten minutes. Do a saucer test. If it sets, ladle into warm, sterilised jars. If not, boil down further, stirring all the time.

Goddess Jam

Ingredients

250 grams / 1 cup each of rowan, rosehips, and hawthorn
    berries

500 grams / 2 cups each of brambles, elderberries, and
    crab apples

1 kilogram / 4 cups of preserving sugar or jam sugar

Method

Sort, wash, and weigh the fruits and roughly chop the
crab apples. Try to get rid of the pips and skin. Put the
fruits into a large preserving pan with enough water to
almost cover. Cook over a low heat until the fruit is soft,
stirring gently. When the fruit is cooked, place it in a jelly
bag (some people use an old, clean pillowcase) and hang
to extract the deep red juice. Measure the juice and add
one kilogram (four cups) of sugar per litre of juice. Boil
rapidly for a few minutes until set. Pour into sterilised
jars, label, and date.

Hawthorn berries and crab apples contain trace amounts of cyanide, hence why we try to remove the pips and skin.

When working with hawthorn berries, wash them and grind them up after the jam has been made, and while it is still hot, fold the berries in before pouring the jam into jars. Use about ten to fifteen berries per full batch of jam. You can cook them, but add them when your jam is nearly finished, and be careful the jam does not start to set before you have had a chance to put the jam into jars. Apple and hawthorn berry jam is nice on pork.

THE JELLIES

When you have cleared your garden and have trimmed the herbs of this year, there is a plentiful supply of mint, lemon balm, and lavender. Make use of all these trimmings and spare leaves by making jellies for the autumn and winter table.

Jellies are great accompaniments for cheeses and cold meats. A lovely, big dollop of lemon balm and sage jelly with a slice of cold turkey or duck and freshly baked, crusty bread is rather delicious this time of year.

Mint Jelly

Ingredients

500 millilitres / 2 cups of water

30 grams / 1 ounce of powdered gelatine

500 grams / 2 cups of demerara sugar

250 millilitres / 1 cup of white vinegar or apple cider vinegar

30 grams / 1 ounce of mint, washed and chopped

Method

Boil the water and sugar for ten minutes, then reduce the heat and stir in the gelatine. Simmer until dissolved.

Stir in the vinegar and mint and simmer for another ten minutes, then remove from the heat and steep for twenty minutes—the longer, the better. After, strain and transfer the jelly into warm, sterilised jars, exactly like the jam jars, then seal just as you would with the jam.

Rosemary and Apple Jelly

Ingredients

2 apples, sliced and diced finely, core, pips, and stalk
  removed

500 millilitres/2 cups of water

30 grams/1 ounce of powdered gelatine

250 millilitres/1 cup of white wine vinegar or apple cider
  vinegar

30 grams/1 ounce of rosemary, washed and chopped

250 grams/1 cup of demerara sugar

Method

Use the same method as with the Mint Jelly. Remember,
the longer you let it steep, the stronger the taste will be.

Lemon Balm Jelly

Ingredients

250 grams/1 cup of lemon balm leaves, washed and
  chopped

700 millilitres/3 cups of water

1 lemon, washed and sliced, pips removed

30 grams/1 ounce of pectin
500 grams/4 cups of sugar

Method
Put all ingredients in a pan and bring to a boil. Pour in the cup of lemon juice. Then follow the Mint Jelly method.

Lemon Balm and Sage Jelly
Ingredients
250 grams/1 cup of lemon balm leaves, washed thoroughly
30 grams/¼ cup of sage leaves
700 grams/3 cups of water
2 tablespoons of lemon juice
500 grams/4 cups of sugar
1 bottle of liquid pectin
1 tablespoon of minced lemon balm leaves

Method
Put all ingredients (except the minced lemon balm leaves and pectin) in a pan. Bring leaves to a boil and steep for ten to twenty minutes—the longer, the better. Strain out

the leaves, then bring the herb infusion to a boil. Add pectin and cook. Stir in lemon balm leaves. Leave simmering for ten to twenty minutes. Pour into warm, sterilised jars.

THE CHUTNEYS

Chutneys are a great way to preserve the fruits and vegetables of autumn. Chutneys can be used on their own or to flavour meat, cheese, and pasta dishes.

Mushroom Chutney
Ingredients

2 onions

1 large red pepper

500 grams/2 cups of cooking apples

500 grams/2 cups of mushrooms

250 grams/1 cup of red tomatoes

1 tablespoon of freshly chopped ginger

250 grams/1 cup of sultanas

450 millilitres/2 cups of vinegar

350 grams/1.5 cups of brown sugar

Method

In a big, deep saucepan, fry the onions with a little olive oil until soft and translucent, then add the ginger and pepper and stir. Add the rest of the ingredients and bring to a boil for at least twenty minutes.

As it's still boiling, begin stirring, allowing the moisture to evaporate through steam. Keep stirring for at least ten to twenty minutes. The mixture will start to become very thick.

A good way to test chutney is to drag the spoon through the middle. If it doesn't immediately fill with liquid, it is done. If it does fill with liquid, it needs more cooking.

When the chutney is cooked, ladle into warm, sterilised jars and cover immediately. Label and date.

Pumpkin and Apple Chutney
Ingredients
1 kilogram / 4 cups of pumpkin, diced
250 grams / 1 cup of sultanas
2 medium onions, chopped

3 Bramley apples, peeled, cored, and chopped
3 tablespoons of chopped root ginger
4 garlic cloves, crushed
4 red chillies, deseeded and thinly sliced
1 tablespoon of coriander seeds, crushed coarsely
1 teaspoon of mustard
500 millilitres/2 cups of apple cider vinegar
400 grams/1.5 cups of demerara sugar

Method
Follow the Mushroom Chutney method, but simmer ingredients for at least forty minutes to ensure the pumpkin is properly cooked before beginning the stirring process.

Don't forget to sterilise jars in the oven while the chutney is cooking.

Plum, Pear, and Pumpkin Chutney
Ingredients
1 kilogram/4 cups of pumpkin, diced
250 grams/1 cup of sultanas
2 medium onions, chopped

3 pears, peeled, cored, and chopped

400 grams/1.5 cups of plums, quartered and stones
removed

3 tablespoons of chopped root ginger

4 garlic cloves, crushed

4 red chillies, deseeded and thinly sliced

1 teaspoon of mustard

500 millilitres/2 cups of apple cider vinegar

400 grams/1.5 cups of demerara sugar

Method

Follow the Mushroom Chutney method, but simmer the
ingredients for at least forty minutes to ensure the pumpkin
is properly cooked before beginning the stirring process.

Remember, the perfect chutney is syrupy and thick,
with no runny liquid.

Plum and Ginger Chutney
Ingredients

1 kilogram/4 cups of plums, quartered and stones
removed

400 grams / 1.5 cups of sultanas

2 medium onions, chopped

1 pear, peeled, cored, and chopped

1 apple, peeled, cored, and chopped

3 tablespoons of chopped root ginger

4 garlic cloves, crushed

2 red chillies, deseeded and thinly sliced

500 millilitres / 2 cups of apple cider vinegar

400 grams / 1.5 cups of demerara sugar

Method

Just as with the previous chutney methods, always fry up the onion, then add the ginger, chillies, and cloves. Fry together for three to five minutes, releasing the aromatic scents before adding the plums. Stir in the sugar and vinegar last. Boil for at least thirty minutes, stirring occasionally, ensuring the chutney is not burning at the bottom of the pan. Ladle into warm, sterilised jars, and always remember to label and date.

Damson Delight Chutney

Ingredients

850 grams / 3 cups of damsons, stoned (if damsons are
   not available, try plums, dates, or figs)

450 grams / 1.5 cups of demerara sugar

A blade of mace

4 cloves

4 peppercorns

500 millilitres / 2 cups of white wine vinegar

Method

Place all the ingredients (except the vinegar) into a pan and
simmer for fifteen minutes. Add the vinegar and continue
to simmer gently for an hour. Blend with a hand blender
for a couple of minutes or rub the mixture through a sieve.
Return the pulp to the pan and cook for ten more minutes, stirring well so it doesn't burn. Ladle into sterilised
jam jars.

THE SYRUPS

The autumn is a wonderful treasure trove of fruits and hedgerow delights that are often overlooked. Yet these gits of nature are crammed with vitamins and minerals and all the essential immune-boosting ingredients human bodies need to fight colds and flu this winter.

In Britain, we have hawthorn, roses, rowan, elder, brambles, and sloes growing in abundance—not to mention crab apples and all manner of pears and wild plums. Take advantage. Go out with several bags and go grocery shopping where everything is free.

One of the best ways to utilize these vitamin-packed fruits is making a syrup or rob from them. *Rob* is an old term that means a thickened, sweetened juice. In modern language, it is sort of an elixir. Rosehip syrup and elderberry rob are two of the most powerful potions you can have on your healing shelf.

Rosehip Syrup

Use any variety of rosehips, but the ones found in hedge-rows are the best (these are wild roses or dog roses).

Ingredients

1 kilogram / 4 cups of rosehips, washed and chopped

3 litres / 12 cups of water

500 grams / 2 cups of demerara or brown sugar

Method

Boil the water, then add the chopped rosehips. Keep boiling for about twenty minutes, then remove from the heat and allow to steep for twenty minutes. After, sieve a couple of times; if you can, use a jelly or muslin bag. Return the liquid to the pan and bring to a simmer. Add the sugar and dissolve gently.

Bottle up in glass jars that have washed and sterilised. Don't forget to label and date the syrup. Use within four months.

Rosehip syrup can be used like a cordial or poured over ice cream and desserts.

Elderberry Rob

Ingredients

450 grams/1.5 cups of fresh elderberries, washed and
   stripped from the stem

450 grams/1.5 cups of demerara or brown sugar

Method

After washing and stripping the berries from the stem,
place them in a pan with the sugar and bring slowly to a
boil until you reach a syrupy consistency. Pass the syrup
through a sieve and bottle it in a sterilised, airtight glass
bottle. Don't forget to label and date it.

Take one to two tablespoons in a cup of hot water
regularly as a preventative or at the onset of a cold.

To preserve and store elderberry rob, freeze it in ice
cube trays and use it as and when needed. Boil water and
pop an elderberry rob ice cube straight in for an easy,
quick drink packed with vitamins and bioflavonoids.

Blackberry Cordial
Ingredients
2 pounds/7 cups of blackberries
6 tablespoons of runny honey
10 cloves
3 tablespoons of freshly chopped root ginger
1 tablespoon of ground cinnamon

Method
Press the ripe, washed blackberries through a sieve to obtain the juice. Place the juice in a pan and add honey and spices. Bring to a boil gently over low heat until the honey has dissolved and simmer for five minutes. Store in sterilised bottles or in ice cube trays. Add hot water to the cordial or leave it to cool.

Black Currant and Apple Rob
Ingredients
2 apples, cored and chopped
100 grams/1 cup of black currants
450 millilitres/1.5 cups of water

2 teaspoons of lemon juice
Honey or cinnamon to taste (optional)

Method

Place apples and black currants in a pan with water and bring to a boil. Simmer for ten minutes, then strain. Stir in lemon juice and honey or cinnamon. Always serve hot. Preserve in an ice cube tray if not using immediately.

From the Cauldron

There is something about the autumn crafts and spells that is especially magical. Perhaps it is the weather and the changes in nature. As a hedgewitch, I find myself creating more spells, potions, and charms during autumn. There is magic everywhere and in everything.

AUTUMN CRAFTS

Mother Nature leaves so many gifts for us in autumn: nuts, berries, fir cones, and the like. It is hard to choose what crafts to make with them. Here are five ideas that have been chosen with the season and month in mind. There are so many projects to do, but one of the main tasks is acquiring your natural resources.

On a clear, crisp day, go out for a walk in nature and collect leaves. Try to collect many different varieties in all shapes and sizes, and make sure they are not torn or bruised. Preserve them using the water and glycerine method (described on page 111).

Mabon Apple Garland

You Will Need

A selection of glycerine leaves

Tapestry thread or wool

Tapestry needle

4 to 5 red and green apples, thinly sliced

Method

Thread a tapestry needle with autumn-coloured wool (red, brown, golden yellow, or orange). Thinly slice four to five red and green apples horizontally, exposing the pentagram inside. These slices can be left to dry beforehand. Alternatively, thread them onto your garland and allow them to dry while they are in situ.

Tie a knot at one end of your coloured thread. As you do, say, "Mabon." Then intermittently thread a couple of leaves with alternating apple slices onto your garland. You can place two or three whole apples on your Mabon garland; just score a hole through them or core them, allowing the needle and thread to go through. On either side, place the leaves. Nuts and whole rowan berry bunches look good on the garland as well.

Make the Mabon garland as long as you want. Use it as a table centre or wrap it around the door, stairs, fireplace, or porch. Complete with a basket of apples.

September Storm Sea Glass Candle Holder

The storms of September wreak havoc on the fruits of trees, especially if you have been waiting for them to ripen. So many times after September storms, fruits lie on the ground, going rotten as a result.

Yet the orchard and forest are not the only victims of these September winds; the sea is shaken, too. The oceans and seas release their secret treasures, and trips to the beach can become another free shopping trip with the wares laid on the shore for all to choose. All manner of things can be found, from seaweed, to sea glass, to drift-wood—and all can be made into a craft project, including the seaweed!

You Will Need
A selection of sea glass
Hot glue gun or craft gun
Large glass tumbler
Tea light candle

Method
The day after a good September storm, go for a walk to the beach and collect whatever you can find. If you are lucky enough to find sea glass, collect as much of it as you can. When you get home, wash it in warm, soapy water and allow it to dry naturally. If you have an old whiskey

glass or a small dish you no longer use, glue the sea glass onto it with a glue gun or craft gun and leave it to dry. After, place a small tea light in it and use it as a candle holder. The light of the candle will flicker through the glass, creating a multicoloured effect. Very relaxing and great for the bathroom.

Samhain Centrepiece

Depending on the size of your table and the celebration and party involved, there are several centrepieces that are perfect for the hedgewitch to make. Buy a traditional black or purple pointy hat and use your glycerine leaves, a tray, and a couple of gourds or small pumpkins to create a wonderful centre for the table.

You Will Need

Witch's hat

An old tray

Hot glue gun or craft gun

Small pumpkins or gourds or squash

Halloween paraphernalia

Glycerine leaves
Halloween lights or fairy lights (optional)

Method
Attach the hat to the tray with a hot glue or craft gun. Glue the leaves to the hat and tray intermittingly. Cover the tray with leaves and place the gourds or pumpkins on top. Anything you have collected from nature can go on the tray, such as acorns and horse chestnuts. If you have a row of fairy lights, these, too, can be twisted around the hat and leaves and lit up during the celebration meal. Go wild with your design and experiment; there is no right or wrong way of doing this. It's all about you and what you want.

You can go completely Halloween and have little skeletons and skulls on the tray, with black and white ribbons and pumpkins all over. Another good idea is placing a pet's Halloween costume on a cuddly toy and making that the centrepiece—this is particularly good if you are having a children's Halloween party.

October Table Mats

There are two ways to make October table mats. The first way involves dried leaves. On an A3 laminating sheet, arrange the leaves you found and cover the entire laminating paper. When it is completely full with no spaces, pop it through the laminator. And presto—you have a place mat that will last and is waterproof. The other way involves a craft gun, autumn-coloured felt, and waxed leaves.

You Will Need
Craft gun or hot glue gun
Autumn-coloured felt
Waxed leaves or glycerine leaves
PVA glue (optional)

Method
Use the waxed or glycerine leaves as templates and draw around them on the felt. Cut the leaves out and attach them, overlapping each other slightly, with the craft gun. Spread them out and make the desired size of the place

mat. You can use PVA glue for this. Make sure you press down hard so that the leaves attach to one another.

You can keep these place mats for years and store them for October each year.

November Scrying Mirror

November is a month that brings mists and fogs, and at this time, things may become cloudy and difficult to see. Create a scrying mirror for guidance and for seeing the past, present, and future.

You Will Need

A selection of autumn gifts (acorns, conkers or horse
     chestnuts, pine cones, etc.)

Gold spray

White paint

Small, framed mirror

Craft gun or hot glue gun

Glycerine leaves

Method

Go hedge-riding to collect materials. Acorns and horse chestnuts, or conkers as many call them, are great natural or sprayed. Gold spray works particularly well with them, or white paint. The colour is entirely up to you.

Buy a small, cheap mirror and glue the acorns, conkers, and any other autumn delights you have found around your mirror to create an autumn frame. In each corner, you could stick a waxed or glycerine leaf.

After it is done, invoke your mirror by saying,

Mirror, mirror, awaken now to me.
Mirror, mirror, show me what only I can see.

When not in use, cover your mirror with a black or purple cloth and keep out of sight so that others do not use it. This mirror is only for scrying, remember, and not for applying makeup.

AUTUMN SPELLS

These are just a selection of autumn spells I have used in the past. As always, they are determined by nature and the weather. Although weather spells can help nature, I was always taught that once you unleash the weather for various reasons, you cannot stop it, and the storm, rain, or wind you have called for cannot be put back in the jar, and you have to just let it blow itself out. Be warned!

September Storm Spell

There is indeed something very magical about a good storm. Although terrifying, with branches breaking and trees being uprooted, the absolute power of nature is wonderful for spells pertaining to career, creativity, or a situation that is stagnant and going nowhere.

Use the power of a September storm to get things moving again. During a storm, light one red candle and, listening to the winds, raise up your hands to the sky and say,

I call upon the lord of winds.
Shake forth that which does not move.
Bring about great change in [stagnant situation].
Move the rock and let movement pass.
Let's get this [stagnant situation] moving at last.

Watch the candle for a while, staring into the flame, and envisage the outcome you want.

October Tree Ribbon Magic

The religion of trees stretches into present day, and in Ireland in particular, the ancient art of placing a ribbon on a branch while asking the Goddess to help in various matters still happens. Tree ribbon magic is one of the oldest forms of magic. During the autumn, with many trees losing their leaves, the art and practice of dressing the tree with your desires, prayers, and wishes for the coming winter or new year is a beautiful part of hedgewitchery.

If you are lucky enough to have a tree in your garden, try your hand at ribbon magic. Tie a ribbon to a tree, saying the words,

Bring to me that which I seek,
oh, great tree,
An' it harm none, so mote it be.

Ribbon Colour Correspondences

Red: Health, energy, strength, courage, sexual potency, heat, fire

Pink: Love, affection, romance

Yellow: Intellect, imagination, creativity, memory, the sun

Green: Fertility, abundance, good luck, harmony, money

Blue: Inspiration, occult wisdom, protection, devotion, rain

Purple: Material wealth, higher psychic ability, spiritual power, idealism

Silver: Clairvoyance, inspiration, astral energy, intuition

Orange: Ambition, career matters, the law

Gold: Money, wealth, sun, happiness, contentment

November Mists Travelling Spell Enchantment

A piece of tiger's eye jewellery is perfect to make a travel safety charm. We travel a lot by night and early morning, especially at this time of year, as the days are short, with dark, early nights. Indeed, November is the darkest month, as December brings Midwinter and the winter solstice; therefore, the sun begins returning to us once more.

Enchant a piece of tiger's eye for your travels. It could be a necklace or a bracelet or even a ring. Hold the gemstone in your hand as you say,

> *Tiger's eye, tiger's might,*
> *protect me on my travels this night.*
> *Wherever I go, wherever I roam,*
> *let me be as safe as when at home.*

Always wear your jewellery while commuting or travelling in the autumn and winter.

The Hedgewitch Travelling Incantation Spell

Mist or dense fog is required for this spell. Do not undertake this spell lightly. Although nothing may happen immediately, when you return, there may be anomalies in time and in your manner, and for the next couple of days, strange things may happen. Always check your watch, as it may have stopped working due to the battery being drained.

Do not perform this spell on a beach and do not perform this spell on a road. You need to be out in the countryside, wood, forest, city park, or backyard, where the fog is dense. It is even better to go camping out in the fog; book the campsite on the day of forecasted fog and off you go.

Walk into the fog and let go. Surrender to the magic of your unknown surroundings. Do not strain your eyes to see; accept the glow of nothing. If at any time you become frightened and paralysed with fear, repeat three times,

I wish to return, safe and unharmed.
Take me back to whence I came, safe and well.

You may not physically travel, but you may experience light-headedness, vertigo, disorientation, and dizziness; see flickers of light; and hear strange music or even bells. This is all normal for the first couple of times you travel, but the more you take part, the easier travelling will become.

As you walk into the fog, raise your arms and palms up as if to receive a gift. Say as you slowly walk through the mists,

> *I call you forth from this plane,*
> *I seek you now here in this place.*
> *Open portals, open doors, let me in through these walls.*
> *Veiled curtain upon the mists,*
> *open the doorway and let me see your face.*
> *I wish to be with your enchanted race.*
> *Travel now into the mists, I call you forth in this hour.*
> *Let me in through the fairy tower.*

If there is no fog or mist, then the night is also a good time to practice travelling, but you do need to be out in nature. Start with your garden and then try somewhere out in the countryside, but always tell someone where you are going and take your phone or, better still, take someone with you, such as a likeminded individual, if you are lucky to know of one. Always keep your physical body safe and use common sense with these types of spells.

AUTUMN ELEMENTALS

The autumn elementals that we encounter during these three months of September, October, and November are as varied as they are marvellous. The elementals of autumn bring the mystery and wonder of this season. There are so many to choose from that it is hard to decide which ones are the most important for the purposes here. This is a transitional season, one that leads to the dark, which is not a negative thing. This is a world of duality, and we embrace all within nature. Just as there is sun, there is also moon. There is night, and there is day. There is light, and there is dark. As such, the autumn elementals have a rather dark and mysterious air to them.

Will-o'-the-Wisp

One of the most traditional autumn elementals is, of course, Mr. Will–o'-the-Wisp. Mr. Wisp does not suffer fools gladly and is rather a cantankerous character, by all accounts. It is often said that in the autumn, he is terribly busy trying to find his lost treasure, which he buried in the spring. Mr. Wisp is often viewed as a "corpse candle," which probably upsets him, too, but he is not one of these. He is his own entity with his own power and really wants nothing to do with humans, and at times, who can blame him!

Will-o'-the-Wisp Connection

If you do happen to spy Mr. Wisp, please do not engage with him. Instead, merely wish him the best of luck in his endeavour of finding lost treasure this autumn by casting a spell for him. As you walk through the trees, say this spell under your breath:

> *Mr. Wisp, fleeting here and there.*
> *Wherever you roam, you do not care.*

Seeking treasure lost,
in a place you forgot.
May this fall,
you find it all.

Salamanders

The other elemental being who begins to make an appearance in these colder months is the salamander, who is a fire spirit and a complete opposite to Mr. Wisp. Salamanders are incredibly friendly little fire spirits who make sure the fire or warmth never goes out in your home.

Salamander Connection

If you seem to be having problems with your boiler or heating, call upon a salamander to help ignite the flame. They will be very flattered you called upon them, as they never expect any recognition for their continued work. To thank the salamanders for always looking after the warmth of your home, light a red candle in the kitchen and say,

Blessed salamander of fire bright,
thank you for keeping the flames alight.

Our Lady of Magic

Queen Mab oversees the equinox with her powers of transformation and knowledge. She is often viewed as the elemental fairy aspect of the Goddess. Queen Mab, in many ways, embodies this season with her shape-shifting abilities; she is as changeable as the weather. Further, Queen Mab is not to be confused with some flower fairy queen. Far from it. She is rather formidable and is known to have quite a temper.

Queen Mab Connection

I wouldn't personally recommend connecting with Our Lady of Magic; if she wants to connect with you, she will. However, a simple offering to her majesty is always welcome. Get some wine and/or some sweet cake (honey or ginger cake is fine). Pour the wine into a little eggcup and cut a tiny piece of the cake. On your outdoor altar or wherever you perform rituals outside, place the wine and cake and say,

> *Our Lady of Magic,*
> *Queen Mab herself.*
> *Blessed Lady, accept my offerings.*
> *Your humble servant, [name].*

Step away from the wine and cake, taking three steps backward, and bow. Then you can walk away from the offering. As you do, take note of what wildlife is around you. You might see a bird or squirrel staring at you as you perform your offering. It might even seem to nod at you. If it does, simply smile and nod back.

Tree Spirits

It is not surprising that the tree spirits really make their presence known this season with their leaves turning an autumn rainbow of colours. All trees have a spirit or an energy that transforms throughout the year. Ancestors knew of these elementals living within the tree, and that is why woodcutters would knock three times on a tree to inform the spirit within they were about to cut the tree down. This is where we get the present-day saying "knock on wood."

Every tree has a spirit who is often viewed as male or female. For example, the silver birch has a female spirit known as the Lady in White—probably to do with the bark of the tree, which is white.

Tree Spirit Connection

If you would like to connect with the tree spirits, perform a tree dressing spell, and instead of asking for something specific, ask the spirit to show themselves to you.

Stand underneath the tree, place both hands on the trunk, and say,

> *Spirit within the tree,*
> *I call to thee.*
> *Venture forth,*
> *and talk to me.*

Knock three times and wait. Be patient; tree spirits can be rather slow in getting back to you. Pay attention to the trees, birds, and leaves around you, as they may start whispering back.

AUTUMN ESBAT RITUAL

When there has been a forecast of a hurricane—and every year we are seeing more and more terrible storms—cast a healing prayer on the night of an autumn full moon Esbat closest to the hurricane or tornado or weather event and ask for healing.

Light a blue candle and waft the light around you. Then say,

> *Healing power of the moon,*
> *cast your gaze upon those who have suffered.*
> *Light their path so they may see.*
> *Grant their passage with safety.*
> *Send healing thoughts and power.*
> *Let them be tendered for this hour.*

Think of those who have suffered, and from the candle, light rosemary incense. Watch the smoke rise to the heavens, sending your healing thoughts upon it.

AUTUMN SEASONAL CORRESPONDENCE CHART

In addition to the correspondences mentioned in this chapter, there are others we can use:

Colours: Purples, oranges, brown, black

Crystals: Obsidian, alabaster, jet

Flowers: Michaelmas daisies, chrysanthemums, barberry, candy cane sorrel

Incense: Patchouli, neroli, dragon's blood

Oils: Cedarwood, clove, nutmeg, cinnamon

Weather: Mists, frosts, hurricanes, storms

Deities: Hestia, Cerridwen, Demeter

Elementals: Fog fairies, tree spirits, fire spirits

Planets: Saturn, Pluto, Neptune

Numbers: 1, 5, 13

Winter

My hedgewitchery days in winter are healing ones. The hectic autumn days are gone, for there is no need to tend the garden and furiously gather all the harvest fruits and vegetables. Instead, winter is the season of rest, recuperation, healing, sleeping, and keeping the family and loved ones safe and close. It is also a season of light-giving parties!

Winter can be three long months of grey, cold days. Yet it doesn't have to be depressing. In fact, these short days with their long nights can be beneficial for mind, body, and soul. Hedgewitchery is about living as close as humanly possible to nature, and we take our lead from the environment. In winter, animals hibernate, and plants stop growing or rest (with some exceptions). Winter is the deep sleep and resting time of the earth, and that is something we need to bear in mind. However, in our frantic world of work, responsibilities, and obligations that we have created, resting and sleeping for three months is entirely out of the question!

Use the winter months of December, January, and February to take care of yourself with spa nights, healing nights, spell nights, and craft nights. Embrace the light festivals, which promise the return of the sun and the promise of spring, with parties for those we love. Use the winter to review, plan, nurture, beautify, and relax.

The winter is the season we feel the weather's harsh hands upon us as Jack Frost appears with painful reminders to wear our gloves and hats. From sharp winter winds, to freezing nights and raging winter storms, this brilliant season is anything but still. The December storms bring hope of snow for Yule and Christmas, while January slopes by on cold, dreich days (*dreich* is a Scottish term for bloody miserable, dull, and grey). As for February, it can shoot by so quickly that you are in March before you blink.

NATURE'S BOUNTY: WINTER

Although there doesn't seem to be much growing in the depths of winter, root vegetables are still readily available. However, with the modern world, we can still have strawberries in winter—but somehow, they never taste the same!

apples, bay leaf, beetroot, borage, broccoli, Brussel sprouts, cabbage, carrots, cauliflower, celeriac, celery, chamomile, chicory, chives, cress, endive, garlic, garlic chives, Jerusalem artichoke, kale, lamb's lettuce, lavender, leeks, lettuce, mushrooms, onions, oregano, parsley, parsnips, pears, potatoes, pumpkins, red cabbage, rocket lettuce, rosemary, sage, shallots, spinach, squash, swede, turnips, thyme, winter white radishes

From the Kitchen

This season sees an emphasis on making zesty marmalades instead of jams, and traditional chutney is limited to just a few extra-special ones. The healthy tonics and teas of spring are long gone; instead, we make alcoholic drinks to share with family and friends.

THE MARMALADES

There is something about the breakfast table in winter that requires citrus fruits. Satsumas and clementines with piles of nuts next to them conjure images of Midwinter celebrations of the past. Therefore, bright and zesty Yule marmalades are a refreshing delight on breakfast toasts of this season.

Marmalades have a basic recipe that can be adapted to suit any taste or combination. From Earl Grey marmalade to Tudor marmalade, these recipes are from my own kitchen and ancestors.

Marmalades can be used with a wide variety of other dishes—great for pancakes, especially the whiskey kind, they are also good on rice puddings, ice creams, and Baked Alaska for an alternative, zesty dessert.

Christmas Tudor Marmalade

Ingredients

5 oranges, cut into quarters, some rind left on, pips
   removed

1 pomegranate

1 apple

1 lemon

1 tablespoon of freshly chopped ginger

1 teaspoon of allspice

1 teaspoon of cinnamon

70 millilitres / ½ cup of cranberry juice

50 millilitres / ¼ cup of whiskey

500 grams / 2 cups of jam sugar with added pectin

1 teaspoon of butter

Method

Put all ingredients (except the whiskey) in a large, deep
saucepan and bring to a boil. Keep stirring and do not
cover. Allow to boil for twenty to thirty minutes, stirring
occasionally so the mixture doesn't burn.

Use the old method of testing jam. Have a saucer cooling in the fridge and place a teaspoon of the marmalade on it. Pop it back in the fridge for five minutes. If the marmalade has set, great; if it hasn't, pour the liquid pectin in and keep boiling for ten minutes, then retest with the saucer. Gradually pour in the whiskey when the marmalade mixture is really thick. Keep boiling until the marmalade sets.

If you like the taste of fruit and there are still some larger pieces of undissolved orange, keep as is. If you prefer a smoother marmalade, blast with a hand blender or potato masher while cooking.

After the marmalade has reached its setting point, ladle it into warm, sterilised jars right to the top, then screw on lids over waxed discs or cellophane tops secured with elastic bands. Decorate with a traditional material covering the top. Leave to cool, then label and date. Store in a cool place.

Like jams and jellies, if the marmalade has not set, boil it again, stirring all the time to remove the excess liquid. The marmalade needs to be a thick, glossy consistency. Always leave overnight just to make sure it sets. You will be surprised.

Winter Spice Marmalade

Ingredients

7 oranges, quartered

1 pear, washed and diced

1 lemon

450 grams / 1.5 cups of jam sugar with added pectin

2 teaspoons of freshly chopped ginger

1 teaspoon of nutmeg

1 teaspoon of allspice

1 teaspoon of cinnamon

1 teaspoon of butter

Splash of cranberry or orange juice

Method

Put all fruit, sugar, and ginger in a pan and bring to a boil. Follow the Christmas Tudor Marmalade method.

Grapefruit and Ginger Marmalade

Ingredients

7 sweet oranges or Seville oranges, quartered,
    some peel left on

1 large grapefruit

½ fresh ginger root, chopped and diced

450 grams / 1.5 cups of preserving jam sugar

Splash of Winter Solstice Brew (optional)

Method

Put all ingredients in a deep saucepan and gradually bring
to a boil, stirring all the time to not burn the sugar. Then
follow the Christmas Tudor Marmalade method. Pour
into warm, sterilised jars and put lids on immediately.

Earl Grey Marmalade

Ingredients

8 sweet oranges, quartered, some peel left on

1 lemon, sliced and thinly chopped

450 grams / 1.5 cups of jam sugar with added pectin

1 teaspoon of ground cinnamon

1 cup of strong Earl Grey tea

Method

Pop the kettle on and brew some Earl Grey tea, no milk. The longer you leave the tea brewing, the better the taste. Put all ingredients in a deep saucepan and gently bring to a boil, stirring all the time as to not burn the sugar. Keep boiling for at least twenty to thirty minutes.

After, ladle into sterilised jars, and don't forget to label.

Ginger Marmalade

Ginger marmalade can be used for all manner of other dishes just like any other jams and preserves. For example, ginger marmalade tarts feature in many Yule menus.

Ingredients

1 pound/4 cups of shredded ginger
2 pints/4.5 cups of water
1 pound/4 cups of preserving sugar
3 ounces/¾ cup of liquid pectin

Method

Put the ginger and water in a deep saucepan and bring to a boil. Simmer for an hour. Remove from heat and add sugar and pectin (if using sugar with added pectin, follow the instructions on the packet for making preserves).

Skim the foam off the top as you simmer for another twenty minutes, making sure the sugar has dissolved, stirring occasionally. Pop a dollop of butter in to stop more scum from forming. When ready, pour into sterilised jars and seal immediately.

THE JELLIES

There is one recipe especially for this time of year, one that unfortunately children cannot have: port wine jelly, a delicious alternative to Christmas pudding if you wish for something sweet and light after the traditional Christmas dinner. Jellies in winter usually will have alcohol in them, but this can be substituted with grape juice or cranberry juice.

Port Wine Jelly
Ingredients
1 packet or 1 ounce of gelatine
½ pint / 1 cup of water

6 ounces / ¾ cup of caster sugar
4 cloves
Blade of mace
1 stick of cinnamon
1 lemon, grated rind and juice
½ pint / 1 cup of port wine

Method

Make up the gelatine following the packet's instructions. Then place sugar, spices, lemon rind, and lemon juice in a pan with water and gently heat until the sugar has dissolved. Bring to a boil and remove from heat. Cool slightly, then whisk the gelatine mixture in and cool for twenty minutes, occasionally whisking. After, strain the spices and zest from the syrup in the pan and stir in the port wine slowly. Pour into a mould or separate jelly glass and chill until set before serving.

Winter Spice Jelly
Ingredients
11 bay leaves
100 millilitres / ½ cup of white vinegar

300 grams / 1 ¼ cups of brown sugar

2 cinnamon sticks

2 teaspoons of cinnamon

10 cloves

100 millilitres / ½ cup of red wine

300 millilitres / 1.2 cups of water

30 grams / 1 ounce / 1 packet of powdered gelatine

Method

Boil all ingredients together for about fifteen minutes, then put on a lid and let steep for fifteen to twenty minutes. After, strain and boil the mixture again before pouring into warm, sterilised jars.

Like the jellies in previous chapters, if this jelly does not set after two hours, boil again and add another thirty grams of gelatine to the mixture. Don't forget to sterilise the jars again.

Cranberry Jelly

There are so many ways to make this jelly, but I always try to find the easiest way!

Ingredients

1 cup of frozen cranberries

3 cups of white sugar

3 cups of cranberry juice

30 grams / 1 ounce / 1 packet of powdered gelatine

Method

Boil cranberries, sugar, and juice for about thirty to forty minutes. If you want to keep the cranberries in, do so, or strain or blitz them with a hand blender. After, add the gelatine and follow the directions on the packet. When ready, ladle into small, sterilised jars.

THE CHUTNEYS

The chutneys listed here are all unique to winter, although they can be made and stored in a cool, dark place until Yule or Christmas. Always use material to cover the lid as it gives an old, worldly charm to homemade products.

Midwinter Chutney

Ingredients

120 millilitres / ½ cup of honey

1 apple, cored and diced

1 pear, cored and diced

2 cups of cherries, pitted and chopped

70 grams / ½ cup of brown sugar

120 millilitres / ½ cup of white wine vinegar

70 grams / ½ cup of sultanas or currants

1 teaspoon each of ginger, ground cloves, and cinnamon

¼ teaspoon of white pepper

Method

Place all ingredients in a big, deep pan and gradually bring to a boil, stirring occasionally. Boil for at least twenty to thirty minutes, continuing to stir occasionally. Do not allow to stick or burn.

Make sure all ingredients cook through and ladle into sterilised jars.

Winter Spice Chutney

Ingredients

2 onions

1 large red pepper

450 grams / 2 cups of cooking apples

3 figs, skinned and chopped

1 pomegranate (use the scooped-out seeds and juice)

100 grams / 1 cup of dates

250 grams / 1.5 cups of chopped red tomatoes

1 tablespoon of freshly chopped ginger

250 grams / 1.5 cups of sultanas

450 millilitres / 2 cups of vinegar

350 grams / 2.5 cups of brown sugar

1 tablespoon of nutmeg

1 tablespoon of allspice

Method

In a big, deep saucepan, fry the onions with a little olive oil until soft and translucent, then add the ginger and pepper and stir around. After, add the rest of the ingredients and bring to a boil for at least twenty minutes.

As it's boiling, begin stirring, allowing the moisture to evaporate through steam. Keep stirring for at least ten to twenty minutes. The mixture will start to go very thick.

When the chutney is cooked, ladle into warm, sterilised jars and cover immediately. After, label and date. If you would like to give this as Christmas or Yule presents, make it at the beginning of December, as specified chutneys need a couple of weeks at least to mature. The best-tasting chutney is one that has been left a couple of months in a cool, dark place.

THE "DRINKS"

Winter, and especially December, is the time of parties and celebrations, so try making some of these traditional drinks, all of which can be substituted with nonalcoholic alternatives. Winter is such a party time, what with Yule, Midwinter (the winter solstice), New Year, and Imbolc, that I have decided to write some traditional drinks we hedgewitches like at this time of year.

Here, you will find old Anglo-Saxon terms like *waes hael*, or good health, in recipes such as Waes Hael Punch.

And an old, hot, spiced ale that was popular in the Middle Ages with the delightful medieval name of Lamb's Wool Brew. The name describes the fluffy white flesh that bursts through the skins of the floating apples on top of the brew. And let's not forget The Bishop, a knock-you-on-your-arse type of drink from the eighteenth-century students of Cambridge and Oxford.

There are also the recipes for Midwinter Liqueur and Winter Solstice Brew. These are delicious alcoholic drinks and are perfect to give as gifts to the unexpected friend who appears only at this time of year, or, as I like to call them, the ghosts of Christmas past!

Enjoy, please drink responsibly, and never EVER drink and drive!

Waes Hail Punch

Ingredients

4 eating apples with 2 cloves stuck in each
8 ounces / 1 cup of soft brown sugar
1 pint / 2.5 cups of medium sherry
1 cinnamon stick

4 pints/9.5 cups of brown ale, dark beer, or Guinness
Thinly pared rinds of 2 oranges

Method
Preheat an oven to 350°F/180°C. Put the apples in an ovenproof dish with the sugar. Then pour in the sherry, adding the cinnamon stick, and bake until the apples are beginning to soften and brown. Do not overcook. Transfer the contents to a large saucepan and pour in the brown ales with the orange rinds. Heat until it begins to simmer, then serve in heatproof glasses, just like mulled wine.

Lamb's Wool Brew
Ingredients
4 eating apples
1–2 tablespoons of demerara or brown sugar
4 pints/9.5 cups of ale, golden beer, or IPA
6 cloves
1 teaspoon of grated nutmeg
1 teaspoon of ground ginger
2 teaspoons of allspice
1 cinnamon stick

Method

Place the apples in a baking dish with a drop of ale and cook for thirty minutes until the apple flesh is "woolly" in texture. Heat the ale, spices, and sugar in a large pan slowly, and do not allow to boil. Strain into a serving bowl, one you would use for punch. After the apples have cooked, scoop the apple pulp out and discard the core. Put on top of the hot ale. Serve hot with a scoop of apple flesh in the glass and eat with a spoon.

Midwinter Liqueur

Ingredients

1 pound / 4 cups of frozen sloes, frozen blueberries, or frozen cherries

6 tablespoons of runny honey

Two star anises

250 grams / 2 cups of brown sugar

70 centilitres / 1 bottle of brandy or whiskey

Method

Put all the ingredients in a large glass jar with an airtight top: a big Kilner pickling jar is good. Give a good shake every day for a week, then leave in a dark place for at least four weeks, giving an occasional shake. After, strain, sieve, and bottle up in small, sterile glass bottles to use as gifts. Leave for a couple of weeks for use, then drink sensibly, and use on your altar for Midwinter or Yule.

The Bishop

Ingredients
6 sweet oranges
2 bottles of red wine
1 bottle of ruby port
4 ounces / ¾ cup of sugar
Cloves

Method
A bit pernickety is this recipe, but it's worth it, especially if you want to get totally trousered for Christmas / Yule. On the plus side, you can make this in two stages.

First Stage: Bake the oranges in a moderate oven for about twenty minutes or until the fruit is golden brown, then place in a large bowl with five cloves in each fruit. Add the sugar and wine, then cover and leave overnight.

After, squeeze the oranges into the wine and pour through a sieve to keep for future use in sterilised bottles.

Second Stage: Add the port to the liquid and heat in a pan. Careful not to boil. Serve in warm goblets and drink hot. Perfect for a Yule party or New Year celebrations.

Winter Solstice Brew

Ingredients

1 litre of brandy

4 oranges, sliced

Two star anises

10 black peppercorns

1 cinnamon stick

Method

Place all ingredients in a glass jar with an airtight lid, like the Midwinter Liqueur. Leave for about three to four weeks, giving a good shake every now and then. After, sieve and place in sterilised glass bottles. Once again, you can give them as gifts. Leave for a couple more weeks of maturing before using. Serve over ice or warmed slightly in your altar goblet for the solstice service.

From the Cauldron

It may seem in winter that Mother Nature does not leave us anything to use for crafts, but that is far from the truth. Her gifts are so plentiful—nuts, berries, fir cones, and the like—that it is hard to choose what crafts to make with them. There are also the traditional fruit garlands, such as dried orange slices or whole oranges with cloves in them.

WINTER CRAFTS

Oranges have always been a staple of winter celebrations and festivities since medieval times, and we have always used sliced apples, too. Oranges need drying, and the best time to do that is on one of those dreich days I mentioned. Slice up at least five oranges or more and place them on a lined, greaseproof baking sheet. Heat up the oven to a warm temperature—remember, we are not cooking the oranges, but drying them out. For lovers of the microwave, this is one task that requires the oven. On the plus side, the house will smell absolutely gorgeous with the aroma of oranges.

If desired, place some cloves in the centre of the orange slices, then place them in a warm oven for two hours before turning them over for another two hours. Slices may take longer to dry if they are bigger and chunkier and if the oven is small, so keep checking after four hours.

Dry apple slices the same way, though these may take less time than oranges, so keep checking.

Winter Solstice Apple and Orange Slices Ornaments
You Will Need

Dried orange and apple slices

Star anise

Hot glue gun or craft gun

Twine or red and gold ribbon

Twig (optional)

Glue a star anise in the centre of each dried orange and apple slice. Secure twine or ribbon through each slice just below the peel in the dried flesh of the slice.

You can tie three of them onto a twig and make a hanging decoration or use them individually as ornaments for a Yule tree.

Yule Star Pentagram Rune

You Will Need

Five twigs of equal length

String, twine, or ribbon

Favourite rune shape

Collect five twigs of roughly equal length and attach them securely to each other with twine, forming the shape of a pentagram. In the central point, tie a wooden image of your favourite rune so it hangs in the centre.

For an alternative, try making a cinnamon stick pentacle. Use a glue gun to attach the sticks, then wrap with ribbon of an appropriate colour for the season.

Yule Gnome Hanging Decoration

You Will Need

Small pom-poms

Red or green felt

Wooden beads
Twine
Craft gun or hot glue gun

Make small pom-poms using white wool and an extra-small pom-pom maker, and trim the edges of your pom-pom—or just buy some small pom-poms from the craft store.

Cut a semicircle of red or green felt and join the edges to make a little pointy hat. Attach a little wooden bead, which has been threaded with some twine, on top of the pointy hat with a hot glue gun, then attach the pointy hat to the pom-pom securely using the glue gun.

The final thing to do is attach a little wooden bead for a nose just under the hat on the pom-pom, and presto, the little winter gnome is complete.

Hang the gnome anywhere—on trees, doors, stairs, picture frames, and so on. Make gnomes in lots of seasonal colours.

If you are feeling adventurous, embroider a little snowflake or rune emblem on the felt hat before you attach it.

Midwinter Smudge Sticks

You Will Need

A selection of dried herbs

Thread

A great gift and so easy to make. If you have some dried or drying herbs around, bundle them together. Some herbs for this are sage, lavender, cedar, or pine. Please do not buy any wild sage or white sage, as it is endangered. Only use the herbs you have grown in your garden.

Bundle the herbs together and tightly secure them with green or red embroidery thread. A good smudge stick is roughly ten to fifteen centimetres long.

If the herbs are very fresh, you will need to wait until they dry out and can be burnt.

Ocean Treasure Yule Tree

Channel your inner Christmas mermaid by creating these seashore Yule trees.

You Will Need
A selection of treasures from the ocean or sea
Craft cone
Hot glue gun or craft gun
Gold or silver spray (optional)

If you live near the coast or have a large collection of seashells, especially the common cockle shells you can find on many coastlines, make a seashell Christmas or Yule tree decoration. However, do not specifically use new shells, as they are animals' homes, and we need to preserve the life we find in the oceans and seas. Instead, if there has been a storm and you find yourself at the coast, have a look at what you can find on the beach—perhaps sea glass, bits of driftwood, and maybe one or two broken shells. Then create this decoration.

Attach the shells to a craft cone or florist cone using a hot glue gun. Cover the entire cone in shells. Some people like to add extra bling by spraying a coat of gold or silver, but I think the more natural, the better.

Imbolc Sage and Lemon Magic Water

Have a good spring clean. Go from room to room and sort out things you no longer need. After you have cleaned each room, make some Imbolc sage and lemon water.

You Will Need
Spray bottle
1 cup of water
3 sage leaves or 3 sprigs of rosemary
4 drops of freshly squeezed lemon juice
Shake up and leave overnight in front of the snowdrops and candles on Imbolc. Use throughout February to cleanse your house of unwanted negativity and guests.

WINTER SPELLS

The winter, although beautiful, is also quite expensive, what with Yule and Christmas—not to mention social-ising and parties galore. That is why making your own alcoholic drinks becomes important and slightly cheaper than constantly buying wine for each party you're lucky or unlucky enough to be invited to.

What follows is a selection of not only abundance spells, but also weather spells. These spells focus on using the correspondences we find around us at this expensive part of the year. You may recognise some, such as the needle and candle spell or the nine-knot spell. These spells are classic spells that can be changed time and time again to suit the needs of the hedgewitch.

Snow Magic

Snow is so magical for us. When the first snow falls, go out and collect as much as you can and keep it in a plastic tub in the freezer until it's needed. This snow can be used in a range of ways, from making healing water, to cleansing and detoxing the house with a spray.

If you are unsure of when the snow is going to come, perform a snow spell using the nine-knot spell.

You will need a white ribbon and a white candle. Light the candle and hold the ribbon in your hands as you say,

I consecrate this ribbon, this ribbon I consecrate.
With the power of snow, this spell I make.

Then, still holding the ribbon in your hands, begin the spell by tying nine spaced-out knots in the ribbon.

When making the knots, say,

By knot of one, this spell has begun. I name you frost.
By knot of two, I name you flurries.
By knot of three, light snow, come to me.
By knot of four, snow some more.
By knot of five, this spell's alive. I name you heavy snow.
By knot of six, I cast a blizzard.
By knot of seven, snow mounts to heaven.
By knot of eight, the snow seals the gate.
By knot of nine, an avalanche of fate.

Blow out the candle and watch the rising smoke. As you do, waft the ribbon through the smoke, and then leave it for twenty-four hours next to the candle. After, start to use your ribbon by undoing a knot at a time. As you do, say,

I undo the knot, send me frost.

Always start at the first knot and never untie the last knot, which is avalanche. As you untie each knot, always say its name, whether snow, heavy snow, blizzard, or so on. Always leave the ribbon for twenty-four hours before untying another knot.

Snow Bath Tonic

To heal and relax during the winter months, melt some snow (use the snow you collected during the first snowfall) and place the snowmelt in a glass bottle with five drops of eucalyptus essential oil and five drops of pine essential oil. Add ten teaspoons of Epsom salts and shake well. Use as and when needed, adding a generous splash to your bathwater. As you soak and heal, say this three times to invoke the spell:

Blessed water, healing powers.
Snow relaxing for hours.

Snow House-Clearing Spell

If your guests for the holiday season have left and your house still doesn't feel like yours, clean and cleanse your home by using this detox spray.

Melt a generous amount of snow (use collection from first snowfall) and place in a spray bottle. Add three tablespoons of salt and shake up as you say,

I enjoyed having you here in my space.
But now, guests be gone, and leave this place.
Cleansed and detoxed, free.
Snow, purify this house, so mote it be.

Spray around the house wherever guests have been.

Popcorn Money Spell

You Will Need

200 grams / 1 cup of light brown sugar

4 tablespoons of butter

½ cup each of cream and milk

Cook some popcorn—microwave or pan will do—and leave to one side. Make some caramel sauce to sprinkle over the popcorn.

Put all the ingredients in a pan and simmer over a low heat, stirring or whisking constantly. Recite this spell:

> *Popcorn mixing in the pan,*
> *send me money in my hand.*
> *Sweet as sugar,*
> *stirring on the cooker.*
> *Popcorn money, three times three.*
> *Popcorn money, come to me.*

After the caramel is made, drizzle it over the popcorn, reciting the spell once more. Emphasize the last two lines of the spell. Then eat the popcorn or share it with friends so you can all share in the money.

Gold and Silver Spell

Collect five acorns sprayed gold and five silver coins of any denomination and put them together in a dish of either metal or wood. Say into the bowl as you stir with your right index finger,

> *Gold and silver, shining bright*
> *Grant me riches tonight.*

Keep the acorns and coins in the dish. For seven nights, recite the spell over them. You can always boost your chances by getting a lottery ticket and placing it over the coins.

The Candle and Needle Spell

Get a long green pillar candle and score it off in five places with a needle. At each line, write the amount of money you need, such as one hundred dollars on the first line, two hundred on the next, and so on. Do not be greedy, as the universe will know. Besides, you will only receive what you need.

After you have scored and written in each amount on the candle, stick the needle halfway in at the first line and light the candle. As you do, say,

Universe, I reach out to you.
Let these wishes now come true.

Let the candle burn down to the first line where the needle is, then blow it out. Move the needle down to the next line and repeat the spell the next week. If you are in desperate need of money, write a higher amount to begin with, but give the universe at least a week to get the money to you. Spells need time to get everything in place!

Money Spell Bag

Get a small golden bag, such as a jewellery bag, either velvet or silk. Inside, sprinkle three pinches of cinnamon, three pinches of nutmeg, and three pinches of saffron. Also, on a piece of paper, write the amount of money you need, then roll it up and place it in the spell bag. As you do, say,

Three times three makes nine.
The money I want becomes mine.

Keep the bag in a safe place—usually with your financial records or credit cards.

Cloud Divination

There are hundreds of cloud formations, and all of them have a meaning. Here, we are just going to look at five important ones that we are likely to see in a winter sky.

The art of cloud divination is like meditation, as it is a technique that requires patience and silence. You are using the clouds to centre yourself and rebalance your mind and soul. And, like scrying with a bowl and water, it expects you to interpret what you see as meaningful to you.

If you have a particular question that you can't seem to get an answer to through usual divinatory methods, such as tarot, oracle, or mirror scrying, try your hand at asking the universe itself by watching the clouds. On a cold, crisp winter day, bundle up and go outside. Ask your question and watch for the answer with your eyes turned to the skies. After you have asked your question, say this up to the sky:

Universe, I ask of you.
Show me the answer I need to see.
Across the skies, show now to me.

Altostratus

Altostratus clouds are very thin and grey. They are overcast clouds but are translucent enough to see the moon or sun through them, though they do not let enough light through to make shadows. Altostratus clouds indicate coming rain and cover the entire sky.

These clouds give the illusion that it may not rain and the sun may shine. Yet these clouds can develop rain, tricking you with their fragility.

Their appearance to you means the outcome you seek is unclear and someone is withholding the truth from you. Altostratus can be compared to the devil or the trickster in the tarot. Therefore, be on your guard, and consider your doubts about people you know.

Cirrostratus

These beautiful clouds have a fine, milky, translucent veil of ice crystals. This can give the sun or moon a halo. It is quite a charming cloud, although this cloud can be an indicator of rain or snow within twenty-four hours. Their appearance in a divinatory reading indicates that your spirit guides and the Divine are watching over you. The rain will come, but you will come out all right afterward.

Your angels are walking beside you. They may have already given you signs, but you have not noticed them. You cannot see the light through the clouds. Think about the past week or so: Have you seen feathers or coins, especially coins with angels? These are signs!

Cumulus Fractus

The cumulus fractus cloud formation is the cloud we see shapes and answers to our questions in. Cumulus fractus can appear as absolutely anything. They are the cumulus cloud that has fractured, and as the wind blows and the air pressure attacks them, they change shape into anything. What they appear as is different to each person.

If you do see these clouds, the universe has heard you and is working on your behalf to resolve things. The universe has given you a great gift…life, so use it. Make your dreams into reality. Do not put restraints and constraints around them. Just do it. You have a special gift called manifestation, and you can use it well. Begin now to see your reality in the world around you. It is not daydreaming; you are not building castles in the air with this cloud. There really is an angel in the sky or a knight riding on a horse in the clouds. Manifest your dreams and make your reality.

Nimbostratus

Nimbostratus clouds are dark low-level clouds that bring rain or snow. Below nimbostratus clouds can lie the fragmented clouds of fractostratus clouds. In Latin, *nimbus* means rain, and *stratus* means layers, so if we take the literal meaning of this cloud formation, it means "rain layers."

Its appearance means that there are big changes on the way that, if resisted, could be painful. This cloud has the same effect as the tower in the tarot.

Before the big changes come, there must be a clear out—a deluge to let everything out, as then things can start moving. Changes cannot happen with a dark cloud hanging over them. The deluge will be over, and there will be blue skies from now on.

Lacunosus

The lacunosus cloud resembles a honeycomb or net. Indeed, its Latin translation is "full of hollows." Further, it is a rather rare cloud formation, or super cloud. It means big events are on the horizon.

It is also a bit of a warning: do not get lost in the big event and fall through the hollows. Check all details of a big event. Make sure there is a safety net for every possible eventuality. Have a contingency plan and a backup plan, just in case. Do not fall through the hollows.

Sometimes our best intentions do not come to pass, and sometimes we fall through the net. If you can, pick yourself up and dust yourself off. If you cannot, it may be wise to invest in some professional help to find the best possible way forward.

Lacunosus represents a safety net and a special occasion, such as a wedding or merger. Just check all details and read the fine print.

WINTER ELEMENTALS

The winter elementals that we can encounter during these three months of December, January, and February are plentiful, despite what some people think. In fact, despite it being Midwinter, the elemental world is alive with magic and is just as busy as in the height of the summer. There is no hibernation period in the elemental world.

Jack Frost

Jack Frost is often regarded as a "bad" fairy due to the cold conditions he brings, but this is far from the truth. He is a necessity in nature; he helps plants and trees, and many vegetables taste better after a good, hard frost.

Frost also disrupts pest and disease cycles by literally killing them off. The soil benefits from a good frost as moisture within it freezes, then expands and splits open the soil—a sort of "turning over" without the gardener having to do the work.

Jack Frost is also a master artist and creates some wonderful patterns and designs on windowpanes, trees, and the world in general. He leaves gifts of magical ice wands in the shape of icicles and creates a frozen world of beauty.

Jack Frost Connection

If there has been a forecast for frost, use the opportunity to gather some frost for your spells. Fill an ice cube tray with water and leave it outside the night of a frost. Ask Jack Frost to bless the water with this spell:

> *Jack Frost of ancient past,*
> *hear my call to you at last.*
> *Bless this water with your power.*
> *Venture forth from your icy tower.*
> *Imbue this water with your gift,*
> *enhancing my spells with an icy lift.*

In the morning, bring in the tray and keep it in the freezer. Throughout the year, when you want to use the added kick of Jack Frost in your spells, use one ice cube at a time. Jack Frost ice cubes are good in defensive and protection spells.

Pixie

We often associate this time of year with a certain jolly fellow called Santa Claus, and his elemental workers are elves. However, there is another elemental being who is just as industrious this season, and that is the pixie. They often get a bad rap, but once again, this is unfounded, as all elemental beings have a purpose, no matter how small. They are earth energies, and, just as everything on Earth, nothing was made by accident. Everything within this universe has a purpose and is connected to something else.

The pixie is one of those strange beings who also can appear in human form. We may have actually met one. They are those people with a rather magical, fun air about them. They might even look a bit like a pixie, sporting the haircut named after them: the pixie cut. Despite what you may think, pixies are actually very orderly beings and like clean and tidy places. They are neat and precise and very linear. They are also very particular about their appearance and do not like a mess, especially with clothes.

Pixie Connection

As the pixie is of both the air and the earth within spirit, there are a number of stones you can use to harness their energy. One of the best pixie stones is fuchsite, which leaves green and gold flecks if rubbed, resembling pixie dust. It is a lovely stone that brings harmony to the home, so you could leave a small piece in your messy wardrobe to bring the balance and tidiness that pixies like. Another stone you could use is ruby in fuchsite, which is perfect for nature spirits and for those seeking love. And another crystal good for working with pixies is green aventurine; this stone is popular and still relatively cheap to buy.

Leave the stone of your choosing in your wardrobe or closet and say,

> *Pixie gift I give to you.*
> *This is a stone of magic just for you.*

In return, I ask this space,
to be clean and tidy, everything in its place.

Unicorns

Unicorns are the ultimate symbol of good magic, for, just like Pegasus, the unicorn embodies spirit. Unicorns are sometimes depicted as having wings, yet many medieval writings and artworks depict them without. Instead, they look like white horses, goats, or ponies with one singular horn protruding from their head between their ears. They do look very regal and honourable, so no wonder that many of the noble and aristocratic houses throughout Europe used their image as part of their emblems and coats of arms.

These majestic beings have often been revered and regarded as a friend to humans. We can find many references to them in the Bible; it is claimed that the unicorn was the first animal to be named by Adam in the Garden of Eden. Further, while we have the serpent as the embodiment of evil in the Garden, the unicorn represents the polar opposite. It is the unicorn who often acts as an intermediary between humans and heaven, although some claim that the unicorn took the side of humanity in the fall from grace and departed the Garden with Adam and Eve. It is interesting that we still know of the serpent, but where is the unicorn? He is lost to myth and legend within the pages of time.

There is a connection between unicorns and winter, as they are revered as strong beings who can and will survive through their grace and divine strength.

Unicorn Connection

If you are feeling stressed and tired due to this busy season, connect to the majestic power of the unicorn by staring at the image of a unicorn on a cold winter night. Light a white candle and say,

> *Blessed winter of unicorn might,*
> *send me strength upon this night.*
> *My bones are tired and sore.*
> *My thoughts and emotions are raw.*
> *Grace me with your power,*
> *all upon this ancient hour.*

Imagine the unicorn power flowing into you from the light of the candle, and feel renewed. Keep the candle burning for as long as possible before extinguishing it safely. Keep the image of the unicorn where you can see it daily, and whenever you feel your strength waning, look upon the unicorn.

WINTER ESBAT RITUAL

You need the full moon for this ritual spell and the coins in your purse or wallet. The power of this Esbat will last twenty-eight days. You must be outdoors to do this spell; if you do it looking through glass at the moon, the money will flow in the wrong direction … out the door!

Go outside the night of any one of winter's full moons and, holding the coins in your hand, turn them over one by one while saying,

> *Esbat power, I call upon you now.*
> *Esbat power, please listen and endow.*
> *Lady of the Night, Lady of Light,*
> *bring abundance to me in every way,*

> *all this month and every day.*
> *I praise the light and work all day.*
> *Lady, send some money my way.*
> *For twenty-eight days, from now till then.*
> *Let money flow to me again and again.*

Keep turning the money over in your hand. Then bow to the moon and say, "So mote it be." After every night for the twenty-eight days until the next full moon, turn your money over in your wallet, pocket, or purse.

WINTER SEASONAL CORRESPONDENCE CHART

In addition to the correspondences mentioned in this chapter, there are others we can use:

Colours: Reds, green, golds

Crystals: Snow quartz, amber, howlite

Flowers: Hellebores, crocus, winter viburnum, daphne

Incense: Allspice, spikenard, nutmeg

Oils: Pine, orange, thyme

Weather: Snow, frost, hail

Deities: Artemis, Herne the Hunter, Cernunnos

Elementals: Snow Queen, Green Man or Spirit of the Forest

Planets: Neptune, Moon, Pluto

Numbers: 5, 10, 21

Conclusion

We have come to the end of our journey through the year. I hope you have enjoyed the magic and wonder the seasons can bring. As we have seen, each season brings a new emphasis within nature, whether it is the elementals or the magic or the weather itself. Every part of this world is connected through the wonder of nature, and we are all responsible for it. No matter how small we may think our part may be, we all have a role to play in the preservation and conservation of our planet.

The gifts this earth brings in the changing seasons are plentiful. And so, feel free to change any of these ideas and adapt them to fit in with your lives. Remember, there is not one way for magic, nor witchcraft for that matter.

You are always in control of it, and the recipes, crafts, spells, and incantations found here are just one way of experiencing and revering nature.

Blessed be, and happy magic-making,
Tudorbeth

Bibliography

Binney, Ruth. *Wise Words & Country Ways: Weather Lore.* Devon, UK: David & Charles, 2010.

Castleden, Rodney. *The Element Encyclopaedia of the Celts: The Ultimate A–Z of the Symbols, History, and Spirituality of the Legendary Celts.* London: Harper Collins, 2012.

Conway, D. J. *Celtic Magic.* Woodbury, MN: Llewellyn Publications, 1990.

———. *Norse Magic.* Woodbury, MN: Llewellyn Publications, 1990.

Coredon, Christopher. *A Dictionary of Medieval Terms and Phrases.* Woodbridge, UK: D. S. Brewer Publishers, 2007.

Crisp, Frank. *Medieval Garden*. New York: Hacker Art Books, 1979.

Day, Brian. *A Chronicle of Folk Customs*. London: Octopus Publishing Group, 1998.

Dugan, Ellen. *Autumn Equinox: The Enchantment of Mabon*. Woodbury, MN: Llewellyn Publications, 2005.

Eason, Cassandra. *The New Crystal Bible*. London: Carlton Books, 2010.

Fallon, Sally, and Mary G. Enig. "Why Butter Is Better." *The Weston A. Price Foundation*. January 1, 2000. https://www.westonaprice.org/health-topics/know-your-fats/why-butter-is-better/.

Forty, Jo. *Classic Mythology*. London: Grange Books, 1999.

Harding, Mike. *A Little Book of the Green Man*. London: Aurum Press, 1998.

Hedley, Christopher, and Non Shaw. *Herbal Remedies: A Practical Beginner's Guide to Making Effective Remedies in the Kitchen*. Bath, UK: Parragon Book Service, 1996.

Hill, Ansley. "13 Potential Health Benefits of Dandelion." *Healthline*. July 18, 2018. https://www.healthline.com/nutrition/dandelion-benefits.

Houdret, Jessica. *A Visual Dictionary of Herbs: A Comprehensive Botanical A–Z Reference to Herbs*. London: Anness Publishing, 2000.

Kershaw, Stephen P. *The Greek Myths: Gods, Monsters, Heroes, and the Origins of Storytelling*. London: Constable & Robinson, 2007.

Leland, C. G. *Aradia: Gospel of the Witches*. London: David Butt, 1899.

March, Jenny. *The Penguin Book of Classical Myths*. London: Penguin Books, 2008.

Matthews, John. *The Quest for the Green Man*. Wheaton, UK: Quest Books, 2001.

Michael, Pamela. *Edible Wild Plants and Herbs*. Oxford: Ernest Benn, 1980.

Moorey, Teresa. *The Fairy Bible*. London: Octopus Publishing Group, 2008.

Nozedar, Adele. *The Element Encyclopaedia of Secret Signs and Symbols: The Ultimate A–Z Guide from Alchemy to Zodiac*. New York: Harper Element, 2008.

O'Rush, Claire. *The Enchanted Garden*. London: Random House, 2000.

Palmer, Martin, and Nigel Palmer. *Sacred Britain: A Guide to the Sacred Sites and Pilgrim Routes of England, Scotland, and Wales*. London: Piatkus, 1997.

Purton, Rowland. *Festivals and Celebrations*. Oxford: Basil Blackwell Publisher, 1981.

Radin Dean. *Real Magic: Ancient Wisdom, Modern Science, and a Guide to the Secret Power of the Universe*. Listening Library, 2018.

Tudorbeth. *The Hedgewitch's Little Book of Spells, Charms & Brews*. Woodbury, MN: Llewellyn Publications, 2021.

Waterfield, Robin. *The Greek Myths: Stories of the Greek Gods and Heroes Vividly Retold*. London: Quercus, 2013.

TO WRITE TO THE AUTHOR

If you wish to contact the author or would like more information about this book, please write to the author in care of Llewellyn Worldwide Ltd. and we will forward your request. Both the author and the publisher appreciate hearing from you and learning of your enjoyment of this book and how it has helped you. Llewellyn Worldwide Ltd. cannot guarantee that every letter written to the author can be answered, but all will be forwarded. Please write to:

Tudorbeth
℅ Llewellyn Worldwide
2143 Wooddale Drive
Woodbury, MN 55125-2989

Please enclose a self-addressed stamped envelope for reply,
or $1.00 to cover costs. If outside the U.S.A., enclose
an international postal reply coupon.

Many of Llewellyn's authors have websites with
additional information and resources.
For more information,
please visit our website at http://www.llewellyn.com.